"Elizabeth has written an engaging, practical book ⌐ grace and power of God and walks us through the jou ration and mending our family tree."

—Kat Lee, host of the *Inspired to Action* podcast and author of *Hello Mornings*

"Laced with pearls of wisdom born of experience and with practical tools to help others overcome, *Mending Broken Branches* is a timely gift to those longing for wholeness. Elizabeth Oates mines God's Word to bring hope, help, and healing to both individuals and families. Thank you, Elizabeth, for sharing your story and your passion for redemption."

—Marian Jordan Ellis, author of *Stand* and founder of Redeemed Girl Ministries

"I love how honest and raw Elizabeth is in *Mending Broken Branches*. She writes like she lives—focused and intentional. Elizabeth has done an amazing job of looking back over her shoulder to deal with the brokenness of her past yet fixating on what lies ahead. In her challenging words she offers great hope for rooting deeply in Christ—the only one who mends the soul."

—Byron Weathersbee, cofounder of Legacy Family Ministries

MENDING BROKEN BRANCHES

WHEN GOD RECLAIMS YOUR DYSFUNCTIONAL FAMILY TREE

ELIZABETH OATES

Kregel
Publications

The author and publisher are not engaged in rendering medical or psychological services, and this book is not intended as a guide to diagnose or treat medical or psychological problems. If medical, psychological, or other expert assistance is required, the reader should seek the services of a health-care provider or certified counselor.

ISBN 978-0-8254-4426-5

Printed in the United States of America
18 19 20 21 22 23 24 25 26 27 / 5 4 3 2 1

To Brandon,
Thank you for helping me mend my
broken branches and create a beautiful
family tree.

To Cecelia and Corbin,
Together, we can mend our broken
branches.

CONTENTS

HOW TO USE THIS BOOK

As a teenager, I felt completely alone. *No one else could possibly understand my life*, I thought. So I went to school every day and pretended life was perfect. I played the role of the straight-A student, the cheerleader, and the all-around good kid. I played it so well that no one would have believed me had I told them about the nights I awoke to shouts and screaming, the numerous police visits to our home, or the time I lived in a shelter for women and children.

Divorce is the cancer that has plagued my family tree for generations, but it is not a stand-alone disease. In my family, divorce brought with it a host of vile cousins: addiction, abuse, abandonment, adultery, dishonesty, financial unrest, neglect, and general dysfunction.

I grew up longing for stability, security, and a dad to call my own. While my dreams were never realized in my childhood, God has graciously allowed me to experience them now that I am a wife and mother.

At the wise old age of twenty-four, I married my college sweetheart, Brandon. Today we have five children, three of whom I birthed the old-fashioned way—Carter, Clarey, and Campbell, who are now starting to ask all sorts of embarrassing questions about that process—and two of whom we adopted through the foster care system—CeCe, our precious daughter, and her biological brother Corbin. We live in the suburbs, I am a cliché soccer mom, and I drive a twelve-passenger van, which has lowered my street cred from hip mom to sellout.

If you are reading this book, chances are we're a lot alike (minus the mega-van, hopefully). We both come from dysfunctional families, we both have dreams that will never be realized, and we both want to nurse back to health our ailing family trees.

But you might wonder how you will ever nourish your broken branches and create a healthy marriage or family of your own. You might hear Effie from *The Hunger Games* mocking you, "May the odds be ever in your favor," when deep in your soul you know they are not.

The bad news is that you cannot repair your family tree in your own strength—seeds planted in past generations continue producing fruit in succeeding generations, us and our children. The good news is that God can change us. He loves to defy the odds and refuses to rely on statistics—He prefers to work with miracles. The God who parted the Red Sea, brought down the walls of Jericho, and came to earth as a hungry, crying baby to save the world is the same God who longs to help you reclaim your family tree.

Why This Book Is for You

You might wonder if *Mending Broken Branches* is the right book for you. Whether a friend or counselor recommended it or your husband not-so-subtly left it on your nightstand, we are all broken in some way. We have all been hurt and damaged by our past. If any of the behaviors or situations below describe your family of origin, you might be the perfect candidate to regenerate your family legacy:

- Abandonment
- Abuse
- Addiction
- Adultery
- Codependency
- Conditional love
- Controlling behaviors
- Criticism
- Dishonesty
- Displaced anger or resentment

- Divorce
- Enabling
- Financial instability
- Inappropriate boundaries
- Incarceration
- Mental illness
- Narcissism
- Neglect
- Suicide
- Trauma
- Unhealthy or excessive conflict

If you are married—whether you are two, five, ten, or even twenty years into marriage—it is never too early or too late to allow God to help you reclaim your family tree. He longs to bring healing, restoration, and peace into your life, not only for you but also for your husband, your children, and your future generations.

While this book directly addresses married women, it also speaks to single and engaged women. Sifting through the shards of a broken past is always a valuable exercise. This book was written for you too.

The perfect audience for this book is someone who, like me, loves stories of restoration. The Bible is full of these stories—Joseph, Hannah, Sarah, Ruth, David . . . God redeemed each of them and then went a step further to send a Rescuer for all of us. If you don't know Jesus personally, I'm excited to tell you this: He came to earth to save us from the very thing that separates us from our Creator—ourselves. Jesus releases us from our sin so that we can become more like Him. Only by becoming more like Jesus can we transform our family trees. God redeemed Joseph, Hannah, Sarah, Ruth, and David—and He can do the same for you.

A Guide for Your Journey

The three main goals of *Mending Broken Branches* are (1) to enable you to grieve your past, (2) to equip you to deal with the present, and (3) to encourage you to build a healthy future. This book has been designed to guide you down a path of healing and restoration. Throughout each chapter you will find highlighted questions. I encourage you not to rush past these questions or think, *I'll come back to this later*. At each question, pause from your reading. Take your time and invest the emotional and spiritual effort needed to answer each question. As an avid journal writer, I'm excited about the space provided both below the questions and in the page margins. Use these spaces to their full potential. Write your words, your dreams, your heartaches—all the thoughts you buried long ago, so you can work through the process of mending your broken branches.

I hope you are ready to begin, because God is ready to help you reclaim your family tree.

ACKNOWLEDGMENTS

Brandon: You always believe in me more than I believe in myself, and I am and will forever be grateful for your support and encouragement. I know you folded more laundry than you wanted to and cooked more corndogs than you cared to eat, all so I could type fifty thousand words of hope and encouragement to women just like me. Thank you for all you did to make this project possible. Without you I would still be a broken branch.

Carter, Clarey, Campbell, CeCe, and Corbin: You are my greatest gifts and proof that broken branches can be mended. I know you sacrificed lots of family time so that I could leave the house or hide in my closet and write. I am so thankful for you and can't wait to play now that all the hard work is done. I'm thinking Lion's Park, Pokey-O's, and swimming. Let's have fun!

Mom: People often ask me, "What does your mom think about your writing and ministry?" I am so thankful that I can confidently answer, "She is very supportive." Thank you for backing me as I share my story and help others who are searching for hope and healing. As you read *Mending Broken Branches*, I hope you see it as a story of hope and redemption—a story you played a pivotal role in, especially the day you took me to Trinity Baptist Church. I was a stubborn, independent teen who thought I didn't need anyone's help, let alone Jesus or the church. I was wrong, and I'm so glad you knew better. Taking me to church week after week was the greatest gift you ever gave me; it changed my life and the lives of generations to come. Thank you for never giving up.

My extended family: Thank you for being my constant cheerleaders, babysitters, Facebook-post–sharers, and blog-subscribers. You read my writing when no one else did, and for that I am so grateful.

My dear friends and fellow broken branches Catherine, Ellie, Elyse, Franny, Hillary, Karen, Krystal, Leslie, Marissa, Martha Kate, Natalie, and Tara: Thank you for digging deep into your past and sharing your experiences, pain, and perspectives in this book. You are brave and strong, and I am so grateful God has linked us together in this life.

Cindy Janecka: Your counseling experience and years of wisdom are invaluable to me. Thank you for providing another point of view that balanced out my own. *Mending Broken Branches* is a better book because of you.

Carly Webb: I so appreciate your editing skills! *Elfie?* I don't know what I was thinking. And you know I love trading stories with you—you always make me feel less alone, and laughing our way through our past is good medicine.

Scott Stanley: Many years ago, when I was a young seminary student, I was trained in your speaker-listener technique. Since then, my husband and I have taught this method to many young married couples. Thank you for creating this tool and teaching countless couples the importance of healthy communication.

Karen Neumair: Thank you for advocating for this project when many said it was too broad, too narrow, too this, too that. I pray thousands of women will find hope and healing because of your persistence.

Shelly Beach: Thank you, not only for your work and expertise on this project but also for your insistence in coming alongside me. You are truly gifted in your craft, and I am grateful God brought you into this project.

Dawn Anderson, Noelle Pedersen, Steve Barclift, Dennis Hillman, Janyre Tromp, and the entire team at Kregel Publications: Thank you for working tirelessly to turn this book from something daunting and disjointed into something beautiful and hopeful—and you made me a better writer in the process. What a gift to be on your team!

MEET MY FELLOW BROKEN BRANCHES

Although I felt alone in what I experienced as a teenager, many girls just like me roamed the halls of the average American high school. Some of them are now my biggest heroes and dearest friends. God has reclaimed their family trees and is writing new chapters in their stories that include forgiveness, hope, and restoration. They will offer stories and insights throughout this book, so I want you to meet them first.*

Catherine ❀ "My childhood was marked by my parents' divorce, abuse, mental illness, and alcoholism. For the majority of my childhood, I was raised by a young single mama who was estranged from her extended family. She lacked basic life-coping skills, which forced my sister and me to care for ourselves and grow up too soon."

Ellie ❀ "I grew up with two parents who never showed affection for one another or me. My father was a borderline alcoholic and verbally abusive. He chose to seek a selfish lifestyle and left my mom for a lady twenty years younger. This caused my mother to become disengaged and suicidal in the latter part of my high school years. Because of the choices they made, I raised myself from age fifteen on."

Elyse ❀ "My family was rich in tradition and had Southern Baptist lineage and deep East Texas roots. Racism was as accepted as churchgoing. Family secrets included my mom's abortion, her mental illness, financial difficulties, and my parents' constant fighting. I dealt with my own secrets of being sexually abused by a neighbor and physically abused by my mom. Today I try to

---

* Some names have been changed to protect the women's privacy.

model forgiveness for my parents, but our relationship requires firm boundaries because they both abuse alcohol and prescription drugs."

Franny ❋ "My mother was married four times, and we spent most of my growing-up years with her third husband. I have half sisters and stepbrothers, but strangely I am closest to friends, who feel like family."

Hillary ❋ "My family was defined by generations of teenage pregnancy, destructive enabling, alcoholism, and mental illness. After my parents divorced, I was raised by my single mom and her live-in boyfriends. I attended school and was surrounded by what I thought was a class full of normal kids with perfect families."

Karen ❋ "I grew up in a Christian home—but not a godly home—full of mental illness, violence, verbal and mental abuse, multiple marriages, divorces, and blended families. Realizing neither parent really wanted me left me feeling empty, and I turned to relationships and alcohol to fill the gaping hole. Fortunately, Jesus saved me from all my hurt and self-destruction."

Krystal ❋ "From the outside looking in, our family had it all. But from the inside, it was a much different view. My father sexually abused my sister until she left home and got married—then I became the subject of my father's unwanted attention. I felt alone among the people who wished they could live the life I had."

Leslie ❋ "I would describe my childhood as having two parts. In part one, life was idyllic—a Christian upbringing, a stay-at-home mom, and a hardworking dad. In part two, everything fell apart. All kinds of hidden sin spewed out all at once, and my family came undone. We have all spent the last twenty-five years trying to overcome that painful season."

Marissa ❋ "I was raised in a family defined by anger, addiction, guilt, and abandonment. There was a lot of darkness and pain in my childhood and teenage years. I was forced to be independent, to raise my younger brother, and to navigate relationships with no idea of what a loving, healthy relationship looked like."

Martha Kate ❀ "To the outside world, I grew up in a *Leave It to Beaver* household that took pride in its Christian values, high moral standards, and perfect appearances. However, on the inside we were extremely broken and dysfunctional, afraid of messing up and disappointing one another, and terrified of imperfection. The last three years have been sown with redemption and reconciliation as our family has recognized that the gospel is not a rule book but grace and love for the imperfect."

Natalie ❀ "I grew up in a legalistic Christian home. My parents taught me about Jesus, but in verbal and nonverbal ways they also taught me that my value depended on my performance and behavior. I never felt loved unconditionally, and I always fell short of the invisible, unreachable goal. I spent years chasing my worth and value in people's love and adoration for me—until Jesus rescued me from that destructive pattern."

Tara ❀ "My parents divorced when I was two years old, and my mother gave my father full custody of me. She chose a worldly lifestyle over marriage and motherhood, and I saw her only once or twice a year my entire childhood. My father was not financially responsible or hardworking, so we constantly moved around. I changed schools at least seven or eight times and attended three different high schools. He remarried when I was five. At times I was close to my stepmother, but they divorced when I was sixteen and I never saw her again. That was a huge loss. And that loss was compounded in my college years when I found out she had been killed."

PART ONE

THE PAST

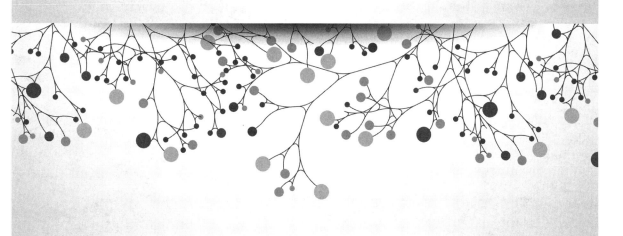

DEEP ROOTS

Finding Your Significance in Christ

The television blared in the background of an otherwise quiet home. I was only nine years old and not yet a Christ-follower. My hardworking single mother sat on her bed paying bills, her anxious sighs slipping beneath her door and into the living room with each check she wrote. My older brother, distant from me in both years and emotional connection, was out with his friends, and I sat alone on the couch. I longed to watch *Kids Incorporated* on the Disney Channel, but cable television was one of many luxuries we could not afford. Bored with the news, I made my way up the stairs to my bedroom, but I stopped after just a few steps. The news anchor was reporting on children and divorce. Immediately my ears perked up.

The reporter is talking about me, I thought.

He churned out the latest research and some dismal statistics on the high school dropout rate of children from "broken homes." His words struck my heart with a chill. That was the moment I realized I was broken . . . flawed . . . second-class . . . insignificant.

I stood paralyzed on the steps, seething at the bleak future this news anchor had just assigned to me. My fighting spirit refused to accept his prophecy. (Being a strong-willed child does have its advantages, so hang in there mamas of tenacious two-year-olds.) *That won't happen to me*, I remember thinking, my anger boiling within.

I will not be a statistic! With that final resolution, I stomped up the stairs to my room.

I've heard and read these kinds of statistics all my life; maybe you have too. If not, let me summarize the popular view for you. Children from divorced families are more likely to do the following:

- Develop health problems
- Have trouble getting along with their peers
- Be more aggressive toward their peers
- Drop out of high school
- End up in prison as adults
- Engage in sexual activity at a young age
- Use drugs and alcohol at a young age
- Grow up to fear conflict
- Commit suicide during their teen years
- Experience teen pregnancy
- Suffer from depression both in childhood and adulthood

Fortunately, my feisty spirit—and God's grace—served me well in life. I avoided those grisly statistics and graduated from high school, college, and seminary. I made plenty of mistakes in my life, but I did not fall into the temptations of alcohol, drugs, or sex as the news anchor had predicted. God protected me from a grim future and opened doors for me that, according to the statistics, had already been shut, thanks to my family history.

Most importantly, when the world told me I was second-string, God told me I was significant.

No matter how many times we fail, no matter how many times our past disappoints us or points a finger at us, our God defies statistics so that the world may see us the way He sees us—as the child He adopted into His family. Nothing could give us more significance than knowing God chose us and loves us with an unchanging love.

It's a Wonderful Life—Really

My favorite Christmas movie is *Elf*, starring Will Ferrell. I know it won't win any major film awards, but there is something endearing about a man who ventures to the Big Apple in search of his father at Christmastime. Not to mention I agree with his four food groups (candy, candy canes, candy corn, and syrup), I envy his ability to feel rested after only forty minutes of sleep, and I admire his ability to decorate for Christmas in one night.

While *Elf* is my favorite, I am clearly in the minority. It turns out that *It's a Wonderful Life* ranks among people's top five favorite Christmas movies. I think most people love the film because they identify with the main character, George Bailey. While I find the movie a bit depressing, I do identify with one thing in *It's a Wonderful Life*: like Bailey, I want to know that I matter, that I am significant. And I don't think I am alone. I believe most people want others to notice them. (Which explains why they post selfies on Facebook and pictures of the perfect pot roast they cooked on Pinterest.) We all want to know that our tiny lives make a big difference in this giant world.

Unfortunately, sometimes life overwhelms us. At one point in the movie, Bailey feels so desperate and depressed that he contemplates suicide. Many people from dysfunctional families can relate to Bailey. As I mentioned earlier, kids from divorced homes are more likely than kids from relationally stable homes to commit suicide. Sometimes these feelings of hopelessness don't go away later in life. In fact, Dr. Esme Fuller-Thomson, a professor at the University of Toronto, conducted a study on this very topic. She found that when most other major life factors remained constant, parental divorce increased the likelihood of suicide attempt by 14 percent.[1]

What circumstances in your life have caused you to feel hopeless or helpless? How have you dealt with those feelings?

Many of us struggle with our sense of significance because we grew up looking at ourselves through our parents' eyes or the world's eyes instead of through Jesus's eyes. As the reporter implied when I was in the fourth grade, the world sees us as damaged goods destined to repeat the same mistakes deeply rooted in each of our family trees. But God sees us as new branches, ready to stretch and grow to provide shade for the weary. He sees us as useful branches, ready to produce tasty fruit for the hungry. He sees us as lovely branches, ready to provide beautiful blossoms that bring hope, truth, joy, and splendor into the dark world. My prayer for you is that you would embrace this significance and claim your godly identity as you start each day.

> *Tara* ✹ I was always so insecure and so worried about doing things the "right" way. In those early years of finding my way, it was so tempting to compare myself to others and feel inadequate. I wish I had been more relaxed and able to enjoy those years instead of being so concerned with getting to the next step.

Trees have historically symbolized strength and identity. Yet many of our family trees looked more like withered, dead plants. God can bring our family trees back to life and strengthen what is weak. It's time for us to reject the Enemy's lies and embrace God's truth. We need to uproot memories that keep us buried in the dry, dead soil of insignificance and accept the truth that we, like George Bailey, matter in this life.

In the Old Testament God told His people, "I am your Creator. You were in my care even before you were born. Israel, don't be terrified! You are my chosen servant, my very favorite" (Isa. 44:2 CEV). God is your creator too. You were in His care before you were even born. Do you understand the magnitude of this? He cares for you desperately, passionately, and lovingly because He has been caring for you before you made your debut into this drafty, wide open world. No matter your family tree or the mistakes that have been made, you matter to Him.

> *Natalie* ✹ Insecurity pretty much wreaks havoc on any and all situations in marriage, and I was incredibly insecure in the be-

ginning. It was difficult for me to believe I was acceptable and good enough for someone like my husband to marry. I think most women, not just me, need a lot of reassurance. And this doesn't make us needy or clingy. It's just how we're wired.

The Trouble with Transactional Prayer

Almost everyone enjoys memories of Santa Claus. Well, everyone except terrified toddlers. Taking pictures with Santa is a rite of passage though, so parents happily place their screaming children on Santa's knee and shout, "Say cheese!"

As a child, I pictured God akin to Santa Claus: I told both of them what I wanted, and I expected each to deliver. Clearly my theology needed a little work.

While I was growing up, my family rarely attended church; we were Christmas and Easter pew warmers. At nine years old, I had no real relationship with Jesus, yet I remember praying for two things: (1) A dad. Any dad. I wasn't picky. And (2) health for my aunt.

My Aunt Patty fought a losing battle with cancer during most of my young life. I prayed for her every night with my hands folded tightly and my eyes squeezed shut. I thought missing even one night of prayer meant God would refuse my requests, so I prayed more fervently the next night and tacked on a little confession. Again, I had major holes in my theology.

Time passed, and I still had no dad. Then my Aunt Patty lost her battle with cancer at the age of forty-two, leaving behind a husband and two children. *Clearly*, I thought, *God is either not listening or He's not there.* I held up my end of the bargain by praying, but God did not answer my prayers. He failed me. So I stopped praying. I checked out spiritually. You might have checked out too, but rest assured God is always checked in. He doesn't step away from us, ignore us, or give up on us (Deut. 31:6). Maybe you prayed but received no answer—or didn't like the answer God gave you. Maybe you thought you weren't important enough or didn't have the right pedigree to receive God's full attention. Squelch those lies and soak up God's truth. If you believe your life is insignificant, lean into Psalm 139. Start listening to what God has to say. Take a few moments to read verses 1 through 6 and write what you learn in the space below. I listed a couple of truths to get you started.

- *God knows me intimately.*

- *God knows my every move.*

KJV.
- God knows my thoughts from afar.

- You know when I leave and when I get back.

- You do not let me out of your sight.

MESS.
- You know what I want to say even before I say it.

TPT
- With your hand of love upon my life you impart a blessing to me — in kindness you follow behind me to spare me from the harm of my past.

After reading this passage, I hope you take away one main truth: you matter. You are significant. God created you. He loves you. He knows you deeply and intimately. And no matter your past or how He has answered your prayers, He longs for you to know Him too.

I realize you cannot change your perspective in one sitting, so I encourage you to meditate on Psalm 139:1–6 this week. Read it in several different Bible translations.[2] Write it as you say it out loud. Pray over it. Let it seep into your heart until you know, without a doubt, that you are loved by a good God who knows the deepest recesses of your soul. You are seen, known, and accepted as God's own child by a God who cares for you and walks with you every step of your journey. He knows you deeply and intimately, and no matter your past or your present, He longs for you to know Him too.

And while you contemplate this truth, don't abandon your dreams. The Bible assures us that God's plans for us are good. "'For I know the plans I have for you,' declares the Lord, 'plans to prosper you and not to harm you, plans to give you hope and a future'" (Jer. 29:11).

Now read Psalm 139:7–12 and write what you learn about God's care for you in the space below.

- *God is always present in my life.*

- *God is with me in the darkness and in the light, in the day and in the night.*

-

-

-

-

-

Martha Kate ❋ "Faith" was a huge deal for my family; it helped develop the legalism and rules we lived by. For so many years I was afraid of messing up because that would show I didn't really love Jesus enough. At home with my family, grace played no part in the gospel, so it was incredibly freeing to go to college and learn that I didn't need to be "good enough" for Jesus to love me.

My early days of transactional prayer (prayers based on my Santa Claus theology and exhausting negotiations) were void of any relationship with my Creator. Even though I was constantly approaching Him with an endless laundry list of demands, my devotion left out this one main truth: God does not need our prayers; *our soul needs to pray*. If I had known this truth—that prayer is about engaging in a relationship with Him rather than receiving blessings from Him—then I might have fallen into a deep relationship with Jesus instead of falling into a deep hole of bitter entitlement and endless appeals.

Yet even in our selfishness and sinfulness, God shows us mercy. The psalmist writes, "As a father has compassion on his children, so the Lord has compassion on those who fear him; for he knows how we are formed, he remembers that we are dust" (Ps. 103:13–14).

Now read Psalm 139:13–18 and write what you learn here:

- *You handcrafted me, poring over every tiny detail to make me exactly the way you wanted me.*

- *You knew every detail of my life before I lived one day.*

-

-

-

-

-

Interestingly, in verse 14 the psalmist praises God not for the things God gave him or the blessings poured out on him but for the simple fact that God created him. God saw fit to give him life. God saw fit to give you life too. God created us. He knows us. And despite our shortcomings, He adopted us into His family. Every day He pours out on us His unwavering love. That alone makes us significant.

What about you? How do you view God? As your Creator? Friend? Father? Judge? What things about your past have shaped the way you believe God relates to you? Explain.

Would you describe your prayer life as transactional or relational? How does this influence your view of your significance, your self-talk, and the choices you make?

Memories and Triggers

According to many counselors and researchers, most people do not remember life experiences that occurred before the age of three or four. If you experienced a lot of childhood trauma, you might hold on to vivid memories at these young ages; or the pendulum might swing the other way, and you might have years of no memories at all.

Memories shape our identity as well as our view of God. If a parent constantly criticized your appearance, those words play like a song, repeating endlessly in your head twenty years later. If you suffered sexual abuse by a cousin while everyone in the family looked the other way, you might have trouble sitting in church on Sunday mornings wondering where your Great Rescuer was all those years.

Maybe you try not to think about these painful memories. You've put the past behind you. You've tried to build a new life and a new family, and you long to forgive and, especially, to forget. The problem is, sometimes our brains don't cooperate with our hearts.

While Brandon and I prepared to become foster parents, we learned about potential triggers that might prompt painful, sad, or even scary memories in foster children. We learned that these triggers could cause foster children to cry; become angry, confused, or upset; throw tantrums; fly into uncontrollable rages; or lash out both physically and emotionally. Possible triggers include sounds, smells, foods, songs, television shows, words, items of clothing, and more. The most random, least offensive object, sight, or sensation to us might prompt horrific memories for the child. Unfortunately, the only way to know a child's triggers is to observe and learn the triggers as the child experiences life.

Adults can certainly experience the same phenomenon. Anyone who has suffered post-traumatic stress disorder (PTSD), abuse, or moderate to severe trauma can react to triggers. Those of us who were raised in dysfunctional homes might be fully functioning, successful adults one minute and incapacitated, floundering children the next.

One year I took a girls' trip to New York City. While eating breakfast (and trying to blend in like a local) at a quaint little deli, my friends asked me about my dad—a topic I rarely discuss. Naturally, when a person is absent from your life, there is little to say about him.

"My parents divorced when I was about two years old and my brother was six," I explained. "We saw my dad on weekends, but those visits were so sporadic and chaotic that I always begged my mom not to send me. My dad rarely forced the issue. He picked up my brother for weekend visits, but I usually stayed with my grandmother." As I talked, I remembered the knot I felt in my stomach every time my dad arrived.

My friends and I finished eating breakfast and walked to the subway leading to the 9/11 Memorial. I continued, "Finally, when I was eight years old, my mom, brother, and I moved across the country, and our weekend visits with my dad stopped. We did fly back that first summer to see him though."

Once we reached the subway, we made our way underground, and I heard the train's screeching brakes. I felt a blast of cold air hit me in the face as I brushed up against the wall. I heard the echo as I talked. Then a flashback rushed over me. I began telling a story I hadn't thought about in thirty years.

"My dad was remarried at the time and had two stepkids, who were around the same age as my brother and me. I remember that my dad picked us up from the airport late at night, and we drove to a house I'd never been to before. He led me to a room that had nothing in it but a mattress on the floor. I asked him for a pillow and a blanket because his house was so cold and damp, and he told me it was late and he would get it for me tomorrow. Then he shut the door and left the room. I knew better than to ask again, so I lay on the mattress and listened to a train go by until I drifted off to sleep.

"The next morning my dad and stepmom left the house before breakfast. They said not to eat anything until they got home, which I now find ironic because there was nothing in the house to eat. My stepsister and I found some sugar packets in a cabinet, so we emptied them into her doll's baby bottles and added water. We drank the sugar water until our parents got home around ten o'clock that night. They brought us Taco Bell," I said, as I remembered all four of us kids scrambling for the food, like ducks fighting over scraps of bread tossed into the water. "That was a pretty standard visit with my dad."

I don't know exactly what triggered this walk down memory lane. Maybe it was the familiar feeling of the cold, dank cement. Maybe it was the echo in the tunnel or the sound of the subway train. Maybe it was the combination of all three. The point is that something familiar triggered that memory—two days out of my life that I had not thought about in thirty years.

You may have similar experiences that abruptly trigger painful memories. Cooking with a new spatula sends your mind back to a spanking that got out of control. A storm causes the power to go out, and you remember all the times your parents couldn't pay the bills so your family lived without electricity. Or perhaps one of your triggers is an anniversary date of a traumatic event.

Memories—both joyful and traumatic—are triggered easily. Difficult memories take us back to places where we felt vulnerable, afraid, unsafe, lonely, angry, unloved, insignificant, and much more. If we are not careful, these negative emotions can overtake our mood and any emotional progress we have made. This is why our minds must be grounded in God's truth.

Keep track of your triggers so you can try to avoid them in the future. And learn grounding techniques to help keep you focused on the here and now for when you can't prevent your triggers. For instance, deep breathing is effective, as is praying, taking a relaxing bath, calling a friend, journaling, memorizing Scripture, and going for a walk. We might not be able to prevent triggers, but we can manage them.

Has something triggered a painful memory and stirred up difficult emotions in your life? Take a few moments to describe a particular trigger and the memory that followed. Then describe how you handled that event. What might you do differently in the future?

I also encourage you to seek a trusted friend or counselor to help you work through the feelings that surface as a result of memory triggers. She can help you better manage future occurrences and move from a place of pain to one of healing.

Corrie Ten Boom, holocaust survivor and author writes, "Today I know that such memories are the key not to the past, but to the future. I know that the experiences of our lives, when we let God use them, become the mysterious and perfect preparation for the work He will give us to do."[3] Don't let your memories hold you back from all God has planned for you, and don't believe the lies associated with your memories . . . cling to God's truth.

Pandora's Box

Most of us have heard of Pandora's box, but you may not know the Greek myth associated with the story.

According to the myth, the gods created the first woman on earth and named her Pandora. They gave her a box and told her it was full of special gifts, but she was never allowed to open it. She eventually opened the box (as if we didn't know that was coming) and hardship, illness, and all the evils of the world flew out of it. This scared Pandora, so she quickly closed the box, shutting hope inside.

This story applies to our lives in a simple way. Our brains are like Pandora's box, full of hardship and hope. The Enemy wants us to keep our box closed so that we keep the hardship, sadness, and torment inside. God, however, wants us to release the painful memories. If we can open ourselves up and release the grief, only hope will remain.

One of my favorite childhood books is *The Giver* by Lois Lowry. The book is entirely different from the movie, which, in my opinion, was a bust. It's a brilliant story of a utopian-dystopian society in which memories, pain, choices, and struggle are eliminated in order to achieve perfect peace and balance. Only one person retains the memories, emotions, and colors of their previous way of life, and Jonas is about to receive all of this.

The Giver tells Jonas, "The worst part of holding the memories is not the pain. It's the loneliness of it. Memories need to be shared."[4] This is true for the Giver, and it is true for us. While the Enemy wants us to suppress our pain, God wants us to release it so we can be set free.

You can start this process by working through the chart in appendix A, "Pandora's Box." This chart helps you sift through emotional memories, process your emotions surrounding these memories, and then record your thoughts, feelings, and God's truth.

Turn to appendix A to see an example. The goal is to refute the lie and replace it with God's truth from Scripture. If you don't have a Bible verse already in mind, you can use one listed in appendix C, "God's Truth." God's Truth will help you combat the lie you once believed. After processing God's truth, fill out the last column by describing your response, or the next step you will take toward healing.

After reading the example in appendix A, feel free to make copies of the blank chart so you have additional space to write as many memories as you need. Pandora's Box is not meant to serve as a one-time exercise. Use this tool whenever painful memories surface. This is your weapon in defeating the Enemy's lies that say you don't matter. It will help you replace them with the power of God's truth that says you are significant and valuable simply because God created you.

Strengthening Your Roots

1. The first time you heard or read information similar to what was listed in the first part of this chapter (regarding the dismal fates of children from divorced families), how did it make you feel? How did it affect your life and the choices you made?

How do you feel reading it now?

How will it affect your life moving forward?

2. Earlier in the chapter, I explained my Santa Claus view of God. What early memories do you believe shaped your view of God? Explain.

Describe how you see God today.

3. What things have triggered memories for you in the recent past? How did you handle your reaction? What would you choose to do differently now?

In what ways would your life improve if your triggers diminished?

You might consider counseling or asking someone else to help you process your triggers. Start by identifying a church or a friend you can contact this week who can give you a counselor's contact information. Also list your goals and how you would like the counselor to help you.

THE PRUNING PROCESS
Discarding Your Heavy Baggage

As a child I believed all married people divorced. After all, both sets of my grandparents divorced; my parents divorced, and every aunt and uncle in my family divorced. I thought that's just what couples did—married, had a few kids, divorced, and maybe even remarried and divorced again.

Then one day when I was about eight years old, I was playing at a friend's house, and in walked her dad after work. "Daddy!" her little sister yelled as she ran and jumped into her dad's arms.

That's weird, I thought. *What's he doing here?* My dad never came to my house at the end of the day. Sure, he sometimes came on Friday nights to pick us up for a weekend visit, but not on your average weeknight at dinnertime. That was just plain crazy! Then I remembered that my friend's dad was a Methodist minister. *Oh yeah*, I thought to myself, *he has to stay married because he works at a church*. Mystery solved.

It wasn't until years later that I realized this man of the cloth had stayed true to his marriage vows because of something other than a career obligation. And many more years later, I realized I had brought some heavy baggage concerning commitment, vulnerability, fear, and divorce into my marriage—so heavy that I'm surprised Brandon could carry me over the threshold.

Step One: Claim Your Baggage

Before I married, I thought two kinds of families existed: the broken and the ideal. After I married, I realized family functioning is not a matter of good and bad, black and white, success and failure.

One of the things that attracted me to Brandon was his love for what I thought was his ideal family—no divorce, addictions, dysfunction, or instability. But as time went on, I took off my rose-colored glasses.

Now don't get too excited. No major skeletons escaped from his family's closet. (I can feel my mother-in-law breaking out in hives just reading this.) You won't see the Oateses partying with the Kardashians or cat fighting on *The Real Housewives of Waco*. Nothing as scandalous as that. I finally understood, however, that none of us has the perfect family tree; even the most pristine family has a kooky cousin in an offshoot branch.

Today, instead of wishing my past looked different, I embrace it. I want to use it for God's glory. I want the world to know God's protective hand is over us, drawing us into deeper relationship with Him even when it seems as if our lives are spinning out of control.

I am broken. You are broken. Even Jesus's family was broken. We strive for perfection. We try to pretend we are perfect. We might even convince ourselves we are perfect. But we are all—at our core—a mess. We all need a Savior to come alongside us and pour out His love on us. We all need Jesus to save us from our sins, to heal our broken family trees, and to save us from the fallen world in which we live.

The first step in preparing to unpack and discard our baggage is this: admitting that we have baggage and acknowledging that the mess we are toting around is too heavy for us to carry on our own. If you want lasting change, ask God to help mend your broken branches. He can, and He will; "with God all things are possible" (Matt. 19:26).

Tara ✸ My parents divorced when I was two, so I don't remember them ever being married. I never felt normal; rather, I felt innately flawed. I even lived with my dad, which felt weird, because most kids from divorced families lived with their moms.

I definitely missed out on any type of carefree, innocent years as a child. I have no memories of ever feeling secure or safe, or that I didn't have the weight of the world on my shoulders. Financial insecurity was always an issue, so we moved a lot. In fact, I attended nine different schools, including three different high schools.

I think this background caused me to value security, stability, and normalcy above almost anything else. I simply hoped to graduate college, stay married, have a job with health insurance, and own a home. I certainly never rebelled in typical teenage fashion or went through a wild phase. Those were luxuries I simply could not afford.

I have always been one to choose the conservative, safe route in life. Thankfully, my husband has always understood this about me. We've always made life decisions conservatively, shying away from anything too risky or too far outside the box. For example, we waited until we had been married five years and owned a home before having our first child. I suppose there have been pros and cons to this approach, but especially in the early years of our marriage, my husband's understanding was really crucial for me.

What about you? What do you wish you could change about your past or your family of origin? Why? What would supposedly be better?

How do you envision your future? What lies from your broken past have shaped your vision? What do you believe God's vision is for you?

Step Two: Recognize That Even Jesus Had Familial Baggage

You and I are not the only ones who came into this world with baggage. Take a few moments to read Matthew 1:1–17.

We tend to skip this genealogy; however, this list is important for us to know about so that we realize that, just as we come from imperfect family trees, Jesus came from an imperfect family tree. Let's take a look at some of our perfect Savior's imperfect relatives.

King David

This guy succumbs to his lustful passions and commits adultery. He impregnates Bathsheba, and then to cover up this atrocity, he orders the murder of Bathsheba's husband.

What I love about the story of David is his multidimensional nature. Before his fall from grace, David praised God, spent time with his Creator, and cried out for protection. After his transgressions, he had a grievous, repentant heart. God extended favor to David, calling him, "a man after my own heart" (Acts 13:22).

David reminds us that we all sin, we all fall short of God's desires for our lives, and that there is always room for grace. God loves giving second chances, if we will take them.

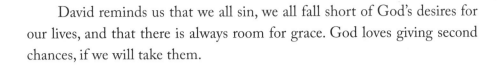

Think of a time you've fallen short of God's desire for you. Were you able to receive God's grace? What did that look like in your life?

In what ways has God given you a second chance? Were you able to embrace it?

Take a few moments to read and respond to Psalm 51.

King Solomon

Although known for his wisdom and wealth, Solomon also gives in to his lustful cravings, just like his father, King David. Solomon gets around more than *The Bachelor* and ends up possessing hundreds—yes, *hundreds*—of concubines. "Wise" King Solomon spends the majority of his life searching for significance through money, wealth, power, status, and sex. In the end he claims, "Meaningless! Meaningless . . . Everything is meaningless!" (Eccl. 12:8).

In today's culture, we see people behaving just as Solomon did—they anchor their happiness and identity to their bank accounts, their careers, and their picture-perfect Pinterest boards. People chase their dreams, achieve them, and then wonder why their lives are still so full of weeds. So they create a new dream. And the cycle continues.

Describe the "perfect life" that you imagine would bring you happiness.

Judah and Tamar

Judah, one of Joseph's brothers, refused to take responsibility for his sons' ill behavior. After the Lord kills Judah's sons for their wickedness, Judah lies to his daughter-in-law, Tamar, and refuses to protect her. She knows she is in a severe predicament now that she is a vulnerable, childless widow, so she takes matters into her own hands by tricking Judah and dressing up like a temple prostitute. Just as she suspected he would, Judah propositions Tamar and sleeps with her without knowing her true identity.

Three months later, Judah learns that Tamar is pregnant. Thinking nothing of his own hypocritical indiscretions, Judah says, "Bring her out and have her burned to death!" (Gen. 38:24). However, after learning that Tamar is the prostitute with whom he had slept, he takes responsibility and says, "She is more righteous than I" (v. 26). In the end, Tamar gives birth to her father-in-law's twin sons. Talk about a dysfunctional family.

The second preparation we take before unpacking our baggage is realizing that even the Savior of the universe comes from a family tree comprised of both strong roots and rotting tree bark—just like ours. When we consider that even Jesus carried the baggage of His imperfect relatives, we realize the depth of God's grace. He allowed this broken family—a family like ours—to participate in the story of the gospel. And we're glad He did! God always uses the most broken and flawed, the most rugged and defiled, the most weary and worn individuals to create the most perfect and sacred story of salvation and restoration between God and man. And that means He will use you and me too.

Step Three: Release Self-Blame and Responsibility

My friend and fellow broken branch Krystal was emotionally and physically exhausted from years of processing the abuse she had suffered as a child. At first glance, you would never know this funny, gregarious, strong, outgoing woman had suffered such pain. Today she has overcome her past and become a victor; she is no longer a victim. But one night, despite the saving work Jesus has done in Krystal's life, she wept and cried out, "I don't want this cup!"

Krystal was referring to a passage in the gospel of Matthew. The night before Jesus was crucified, He sat and prayed in the garden of Gethsemane. Scripture tells us He felt so overwhelmed by the task before Him that He "fell with his face to the ground and prayed, 'My Father, if it is possible, may this cup be taken from me. Yet not as I will, but as you will'" (Matt. 26:39).

When Jesus said, "this cup," He was referring to God's wrath. Jesus knew He was about to take on God's judgment meant for the whole world. When we, like Krystal, suffer hardships such as abuse, abandonment, neglect, and more, it can feel as if we are suffering judgment, punishment, or wrath from God, but the truth is that Jesus took the punishment that belongs to our perpetrator. Adversities such as sexual abuse do not occur because we deserve them or because they are a result of God's judgment. They happen as a result of living in a fallen world with fallen people, who have the freedom to make corrupt choices.

The next step in preparing to unpack your baggage is accepting the fact that you did nothing wrong to deserve the harsh treatment you endured while growing up. Releasing self-blame takes lots of time and emotional work. It requires understanding, empathy, forgiveness, and healing—all of which I'm helping you work toward in this book. To get started, here are a few tips:

- When you blame yourself for something in the past, repeat these words: "I was a child. I did not deserve what happened to me. I was innocent and blameless and bear no responsibility." Continue repeating this truth (or a similar truth) until the negative thought passes.
- Avoid the people or situations causing you to feel responsible for past hurts that were not your fault.
- Stop punishing yourself through negative self-talk, self-harm, isolation, binging and purging, and other destructive behaviors. That is easier said than done, so seek out a counselor or mentor to help you identify and work through these issues.

Natalie ✳ I often thought, It's me. I'm not lovable for some reason. It's taken years of counseling and believing God's word to help me recognize what is my responsibility and what is not.

We don't have the luxury of choosing our circumstances, but we do have the ability to choose our responses to our circumstances. We don't have the ability to choose our story, but we do have the privilege of choosing what we will do with it. We can run from it or embrace it. We can ignore it or use it to help others. We can allow the Enemy to take control of our lives, or we can use our testimony for God's glory.

The most encouraging thing about Krystal's story is that it doesn't end with her abuse. She has unpacked her bag of shame and guilt, and through the healing power of Jesus, she has created a beautiful family and positively influenced many people in her life. This is my hope for you too.

Step Four: Deconstruct Your Past

Professor Jean M. Twenge writes, "Talk shows, psychoanalytic therapy, and books all encourage us to analyze just how our 'dysfunctional family' has damaged us."[1] She also asserts that blaming our parents has become a national obsession.

Please hear my heart. I do not believe every family is dysfunctional—imperfect, yes, but not dysfunctional. I also do not believe that every adult should blame their parents for their failures, their fears, or their shortcomings. Blaming families is *not* my goal in writing this book, and I hope blaming others is not your goal either. Blaming others—including God—will not bring the healing and restoration we need. I do, however, believe in the value of deconstructing our past so we can build a healthier future for ourselves, our marriages, and our children.

The purpose of this book—and the next exercise—is to help you uproot past patterns of brokenness or dysfunction that have influenced your family. Now that you know how to unpack your heavy baggage, you are ready to move forward. To help you do this, I have provided the Deconstruction for Reconstruction chart found in appendix B. (Just as with the other charts, you might want to make copies before you write in the book so you can continue adding to the list as needed.)

Here is how the chart works: In the left-hand column, marked "Deconstruction," write a dysfunctional characteristic (baggage) from your family of origin that you want to leave behind. Then in the second column write how this behavior affected you or made you feel, or a lie you believed because of it. In the third column, labeled "God's Truth," use the Bible verses I provided in appendix C (just as you did for your Pandora's Box chart). This allows you to shine biblical truth and light on the darkness you experienced while growing up. In the last column, "Reconstruction," write your response to God's truth. This is your chance to assert power over the dysfunction. You will also make an action plan to help you release the weight of the baggage that has weighed you down. Appendix B provides an example chart as well as a blank chart for you to fill in. Feel free to turn there now and get started before reading the rest of this chapter.

Step Five: Let Go of Old Ways

The Bible often uses building metaphors to reveal God's truth. While I realize we're not all in the construction business, my guess is that many of us watch HGTV. If you live in Waco, like me, watching *Fixer Upper* is practically a city ordinance (#shiplap #demoday). Whether or not you watch home improvement shows, I think we can all relate to the idea of wanting to create or build something beautiful. The millions of women perusing Pinterest and Houzz while thinking their newly remodeled kitchen makes them the next big thing since Chip and Joanna Gaines tells me I'm right.

Jesus was a carpenter by trade, so He understands the importance of building something on a strong foundation, both in construction and in life.

> These words I speak to you are not incidental additions to your life, homeowner improvements to your standard of living. They are foundational words, words to build a life on. If you work these words into your life, you are like a smart carpenter who built his house on solid rock. Rain poured down, the river flooded, a tornado hit—but nothing moved that house. It was fixed to the rock.
>
> But if you just use my words in Bible studies and don't work them into your life, you are like a stupid carpenter who built his house on the sandy beach. When a storm rolled in and the waves came up, it collapsed like a house of cards. (Matt. 7:24–27 MSG)

Building a life based on Jesus—not our family history—requires us to love Jesus more than we love ourselves—to look more like Jesus and less like ourselves. We must pursue Jesus individually and with our spouses and constantly ask God how He wants our lives to look. We accomplish this by studying God's Word and then living out what it says. We are called to love and respect our husband while finding confidence in our place in the marriage. We should love our children and teach them God's Word. We should pursue Christlike community and serve others not at a once-a-year service project but as we move through our days and weeks and years. In other words, we're not merely changing a paint color or adding on a room—we're building a life!

Strengthening Your Roots

1. What baggage weighs you down (a painful memory, a strained relationship, your emotions toward a family member, how your difficult childhood has manifested itself today, etc.)? Describe it here.

What prevents you from unpacking this baggage (i.e., what prevents you from working through this issue and reaching a point of healing)?

2. What do the stories of David, Solomon, and Judah and Tamar teach you about—
   Yourself?

   Your family of origin?

   God?

3. Have you ever felt as if you were partly to blame for something specific that
   occurred while you were growing up or the general dysfunction in your family?
   Explain.

4. After reading Krystal's story, are you better able to accept the fact that you did nothing to deserve the treatment you endured while growing up? Explain.

5. In this chapter I wrote, "We don't have the luxury of choosing our circumstances, but we do have the ability to choose our responses to our circumstances. We don't have the ability to choose our story, but we do have the privilege of choosing what we will do with it. We can run from it or embrace it. We can ignore it or use it to help others. We can allow the Enemy to take control of our lives, or we can use our testimony for God's glory." Are you in a place, emotionally and spiritually, where you can use your story to help others and to further God's kingdom? If so, how will you do it? If not, ask God to move you to that point of healing so that your suffering will help others experience God's healing.

WEEPING WILLOWS
Creating Space to Grieve

The summer I was pregnant with my first child, insecurities about my impending motherhood surfaced as I recalled my own childhood and relationship with my mom. Like many children with divorced parents, my heart ached over the intangible things I missed while growing up. My mom did a great job when it came to celebrating holidays, allowing us to participate in various activities, teaching me the fine art of bargain shopping, and making sure we received a quality education. But single motherhood is a difficult and demanding job that is emotionally, mentally, and financially draining. As a result, I often felt hurt and lonely.

As I prepared to become a mom, I needed to process some of those feelings, so I met with a woman named Joye who was an adjunct professor at the seminary I attended. She was wise, patient, and calm—all of the things I knew I would never be as a mother but desperately wanted to be. The first day I met with her I poured out my heart (and used an entire box of tissues). I relived the pain from my past and confessed my fears of the future. After our first meeting she graciously agreed to meet with me again. And again. And again. Our few meetings soon turned into weekly meetings.

Finally one day Joye told me, "Elizabeth, in order to move forward, you have to grieve the childhood you always wanted." I finally accepted the fact that life is not fair, and contrary to what our culture tries to make us believe, God never designed it to be this way.

Thanks to Joye, I've let go of my pain and unrealized dreams. I envisioned the kind of mom *I wanted to become*: the mom who assures her children they are significant, not because of what they do or accomplish but simply because they exist and breathe and take up space in this world. The mom who comforts her children when they wither and encourages them when they bloom. The mom who loves her children unconditionally, even when they make a mess, wreck the car, fail the big test, say hurtful things, or don't get into their dream college—especially when these things occur, because that is why unconditional love exists. Joye gave me permission to grieve my past and the ability to embrace my future motherhood with confidence.

The Importance of Grieving Your Past

One of my favorite movies when I was growing up was *My Girl*, the coming-of-age story about an eleven-year-old girl, Vada Sultenfuss, who is raised in a funeral home by her single dad. Vada is best friends with Thomas J., a bookish boy. Together they ride bikes, climb trees, and try to understand life. Vada also avoids the reality that her widower father is falling in love.

In a tragic accident, Thomas J. dies, leaving Vada to grieve the loss of her only friend. I remember watching the scene where Vada crashes Thomas J.'s funeral. I cried as if I were attending the funeral myself—as if Thomas J. were my own lifelong friend.

"Come back, Thomas J.! Come back!" Vada cried over the casket. Oh my stars, I can hardly take it, even today. Our deep-feeling heroine turns to poetry to process her feelings, and young Vada writes a poem about the weeping willow she and Thomas J. spent so much time climbing. The funeral, the tears, the poem—all were a part of the grieving process for Vada.

Just as we see in *My Girl*, there are many reasons to embrace grief and pursue our own journey from denial to acceptance. Pain and loss were never a part of God's original plan. Just as childhood death was never God's design, neither was the dysfunction you experienced as a child. God grieves the pain in your past, and He wants you to grieve as well.

Vada lost her mother and her best friend, and the audience watches a young girl process deep grief. We wonder how God can ever work such grief out for good. Eventually, however, He does. He can take a sad, broken little girl, and teach her that it's OK to feel. It's OK to love. It's OK to open your heart to possibility.

It might not seem so in the moment, but just like Vada, we can always look back on our lives and realize that even in the darkest situations, God always works out painful events for our good (Rom. 8:28). If we ever forget this truth, we need only remember Jesus's suffering and death on the cross as a case in point.

Another thing to remember as you grieve your past is that pain is a universal experience. You are not alone in your anguish; everyone experiences disappointment, pain, suffering, and loss at some point in their lives—even Jesus felt it. "So he was despised and forsaken by men, this man of suffering, grief's *patient* friend. As if he was a person to avoid, we looked the other way; he was despised, *forsaken*, and we took no notice of him" (Isa. 53:3 voice).

Finally, God sanctifies us through our grief. In pain and suffering we can run from Jesus or we can try to respond like Him and in the end look more like Him. King Solomon wrote about this principle:

> It is better to go to a house of mourning
> than to go to a house of feasting,
> for death is the destiny of everyone;
> the living should take this to heart.
> (Eccl. 7:2)

If we accept the truth that our reality will look nothing like the dreams we've conjured up, then we can move forward and grieve the pain, suffering, and lost opportunities—all that should have and could have been—even all that might have been ours. But you won't be alone with your grief—Jesus sent the Holy Spirit to comfort you.

And I will ask the Father, and he will give you another advocate to help you and be with you forever—the Spirit of truth. The world cannot accept him, because it neither sees him nor knows him. But you know him, for he lives with you and will be in you. I will not leave you as orphans; I will come to you. Before long, the world will not see me anymore, but you will see me. Because I live, you also will live. On that day you will realize that I am in my Father, and you are in me, and I am in you. (John 14:16–20)

Why do you think God wants you to grieve your past? Is it because of one of the reasons listed above or an entirely different reason? Explain.

Grieving Your Lost Childhood

School had always been my escape—the place I went to avoid the chaos at home. Every day, after learning math facts and diagramming sentences, I arrived home to turmoil and trepidation. In third grade I attended a new school in a new city, but as soon as we moved into a new apartment, we had to move out again. With no place else to go, we moved into a small apartment with another family. The situation was not safe or stable, but it was shelter.

Despite my home life, I always knew I was destined for stardom. Don't ask me where I got that idea. Maybe it was all those Shirley Temple movies I watched with my grandmother when I was younger. I couldn't sing; I had no acting experience; and I had taken only one year of ballet, but I knew the stage was beckoning me.

So imagine my delight when I was one of ten girls chosen to be a snowflake in our school's Christmas play, *The Nutcracker*. This was a huge honor because it was a play starring fourth and fifth graders. But everyone knows snowflakes are tiny, delicate, fragile things, so the teachers recruited younger girls to play this important role in the show. I forfeited weeks of recess to rehearse at school, and I practiced my choreographed dance at home. I counted down the days until my off-off-off Broadway debut—until days before I was scheduled to perform when, once again, we found ourselves with no place to live. The circumstances were traumatic, and our future was uncertain.

My mom needed time to get her life in order, so she sent my brother and me across the country to stay with extended family. Saying goodbye to everything familiar was frightening enough, but what hurt me the most was losing my dream role in *The Nutcracker*. I remember feeling crushed by having to give up my custom-made costume, having to waste the hours of practice, and having my shining moment snatched away. At the time, it didn't feel as if I had permission to shed tears or give voice to my disappointment, so I acted brave and obedient and watched silently as my chance to be a star—even if for only one night—was given to another third grader. I learned at an early age that I wasn't special after all; I was replaceable. I held on to my disappointment for years—until I learned how to grieve the childhood I had lost.

What example of forfeiting a piece of your childhood can you recall?

Comparing Your Dream and Your Reality

I remember watching *The Brady Bunch* and dreaming about what it would be like to join their family (of course that's before I knew Carol Brady was having an off-camera affair with her TV son Greg—awkward!). I loved all the chaos, the energy, the family games (who could forget the potato sack race), and the family musicals! (Remember, I was destined for stardom.)

Maybe you dreamed about a childhood that looked completely different from your reality. Maybe you painted a utopian portrait in your mind, but it never came true. Or maybe you never allowed yourself the luxury of daydreaming. Either way, this is your chance to process your dreams and losses for a few moments, and then answer the questions below. If you could create a dream childhood . . .

Who would live with you?

Where would you live?

What would you do in your idyllic childhood?

How would you feel?

If you are reading this book, there's no doubt your perfect childhood and your reality looked drastically different from each other. A maid like Alice never baked homemade cookies for you after school. A father like Mike Brady never had a heart-to-heart with you in his study. A brother like Bobby Brady never played ping-pong with you in the driveway.

After my snowflake dreams melted, my family's branches continued to break. Even so, I continued to dream.

Fast-forwarding to my middle school years, my mom remarried, and I thought our tumultuous journey was over. I hoped her new marriage would be the dream I had waited for.

Unfortunately, in my newly blended family, fighting, tension, conditional love, and other forms of dysfunction ensued. I vacillated between striving to earn love and attention, and trying to remain invisible just to keep the peace. No matter how hard I tried to please, I failed. I began to feel defeated, like the weeping willow that has no strength to lift its branches. This lasted a couple of years until one night when years of volatility reached a new level and I saw evil with my own eyes. My mom and stepdad's marriage came to a sudden end. Our family became undone. I was only a ninth grader, and my life was a mess. Our family became fodder for small-town gossip. We were once again broken branches. My pipe dream had ended. My reality continued.

Think back to your childhood reality and take some time to answer the following questions.

Who lived with you?

Where did you live?

What were the relational dynamics between your family members?

What was the atmosphere like in your home?

How did you respond?

How did you feel? (loved, safe, secure, afraid, lonely, happy, unhappy, valued, neglected, weary, sad, insignificant)?

If you could change one thing about your childhood reality, what would it be?

Natalie ✿ I imagined a life that was far from my childhood life. I wanted to be independent, wild, free, and alone. I've been equally disappointed and grateful that the dream scenario I had pictured didn't come true.

Five Stages of Grief

Now that we know *why* we should grieve and *what* we are grieving, we need a roadmap to help us work our way through our grief. The five stages of grief are just that, but keep in mind that we don't always walk through these stages with linear progression. We might skip steps and circle back to them; we might leave steps out altogether. We might complete the final stage—acceptance—only to find ourselves regressing back to one of the earlier stages of grief that we passed through months or even years earlier. It's difficult to predict where our emotions and experiences will take us.

Give yourself permission to ebb and flow through the various stages of grief. Don't let anyone tell you how you should feel at any given moment. Give yourself the emotional time and space you need to experience all the stages, so you can come to a place of wholeness and healing.

1. Denial

We refuse to admit to ourselves or others that the problem or situation exists—or the severity of the crisis. We emotionally numb and protect ourselves from the intense pain. For instance, by not telling your friends that your dad drank all the time, or that your parents divorced, you escaped to a peaceful fantasy world. Unfortunately, denial is an emotional volcano that remains dormant for only so long—the volcano eventually erupts.

> For there is nothing hidden that will not be disclosed, and nothing concealed that will not be known or brought out into the open. (Luke 8:17)

Recall a time when you refused to admit something to yourself or others. How did keeping it a secret make the situation worse?

2. Anger

We feel helpless, powerless, abandoned, or cheated out of something we think we deserve—everything feels out of our control. Type A personalities might find themselves stuck in the anger phase for a very long time, as entitlement runs deep. (Not that I would know anything about that. Ahem.) We can become angry with ourselves, with others, and with God. We ask questions such as, "Why me?" and "How could this happen?" And we make statements such as, "It's not fair!" If we feel angry with God, we say, "How could you let this happen?"

> My dear brothers and sisters, take note of this: Everyone should be quick to listen, slow to speak and slow to become angry. (James 1:19)

How do you handle anger? How does the way you deal with your anger affect others?

3. Bargaining

We wrestle, thinking about what might have been. If our parents were overly critical of us or neglected us, we wonder why we weren't enough. "If only I had been a better athlete, a better student, or Homecoming Queen, things would have been different," we say, creating false scenarios in our minds, shifting the burden of responsibility from our parents or other responsible adults to ourselves.

> Each one should carry their own load. (Gal. 6:5)

In what ways do you shoulder the burden of problems in your family of origin and try to carry everyone's load?

What are the consequences of this for your health? Your emotions? Your own family? Your relationships? Your schedule?

---

4. Depression

We feel sad, lonely, powerless, lost, and hopeless. We realize the depth of our situation and recognize that we cannot change the past, so we give up. We disconnect from others in order to avoid getting hurt by yet another person. Like a weeping willow, we become limp and frail, and we give up.

> When you go through deep waters, I will be with you. When you go through rivers of difficulty, you will not drown. When you walk through the fire of oppression, you will not be burned up; the flames will not consume you. (Isa. 43:2 NLT)

People experience depression along a wide spectrum, from mild sadness to full blown I-can't-get-out-of-bed-for-days despair. Describe a time when you or a family member has dealt with depression. What did it look and feel like? What helped bring you or them out of it?

If you or someone you know has fallen into depression, please seek help. Medications and counselors can help lead people out of despair (more on this later in the chapter).

5. Acceptance

We acknowledge the past for what it is. We no longer remain immersed in our pain or wish for a different ending. We accept our story and the God who wrote it.

This is our goal, friends: to move to a place of acceptance. You might not be there yet, and that's OK. We are on this journey together, and you are just beginning.

Whether or not you have reached the acceptance stage, describe what the acceptance stage looks like for you.

Practically Speaking, How Do You Grieve?

I am a very pragmatic person. I like instructions and bullet points and to-do lists. So it's not enough for me to know the five stages of grief. I need to know *how* to work through the stages. If you're like me, you'll like this next section so much you might buy me a Starbucks gift card or offer to babysit my children (both of which I will gladly accept).

First, *pour out your heart to God*—He already knows what you are thinking and feeling, but there is something cathartic and healing about voicing our thoughts and emotions to Him. "Cast all your anxiety on him because he cares for you" (1 Peter 5:7). When you share your anxieties and grief with God, you will no doubt feel a wave of comfort. "The Lord is close to the brokenhearted and saves those who are crushed in spirit" (Ps. 34:18).

Next, *rely on your community*, which might include your husband, family, friends, church, life group, or neighbor. Your community is any like-minded person or group of people who will pray for you and with you and walk you through this difficult time. "Carry each other's burdens, and in this way you will fulfill the law of Christ" (Gal. 6:2).

Finally, *ignore the Enemy*. He knows when you are weak and vulnerable, and he will try to take advantage of you. Arm yourself with God's Word and cling to the truth that you know. "Be alert and of sober mind. Your enemy the devil prowls around like a roaring lion looking for someone to devour" (1 Peter 5:8).

As Joye taught me, you need to let go of the childhood and family you desperately wanted but never experienced: the mom who baked cupcakes, the dad who let you dance on his feet, and the family movie nights.

Surrendering a desire this precious is a like a death—it is in fact the death of what you thought your life should look like. It is the death of what you thought you deserved. It's not easy to say, "God, you did not give me the life I wanted, but I trust you will work out my life for my good and for your glory." If you have never grieved the loss of what you hoped for, I urge you to take some time to do that.

Natalie ❀ I have grieved and continue to grieve the loss of the parents I always wanted. Grief comes at odd times—like when leaving a parent-teacher conference and longing to call my parents and ask what to do or if this same situation happened to them. However, there are times when I expect grief, but it doesn't wash over me. I think it's all part of the grieving process.

Walking through the grieving process looks different for everyone. For me, it means sitting in a quiet place and feeling the range of emotions associated with a particular situation. After a lot of questioning and crying and calling out to God, I bring myself back to the truth I know: God has always worked out tough situations for my benefit—whether to teach me something, make me stronger, or draw me closer to Him. No matter what happens, I know that I serve a good God who has a good plan for my life. I also remind myself of the person God has molded me into as a result of my past, knowing He has not wasted a drop of my pain. "We know that in all things God works for the good of those who love him, who have been called according to his purpose" (Rom. 8:28). Then I give thanks for all the blessings He has heaped upon me, because I realize I don't deserve even one of them.

For other people, grieving might include reading Scripture and journaling. They might listen to worship music and pray, or they might take their questions and concerns to a pastor, counselor, or trusted friend. Remember, the grieving process is not a sitcom; it does not reach resolution in one thirty-minute session. It takes time for you to fully process your range of thoughts and emotions. So feel free to take some time to grieve the childhood you dreamed of, the parents you wanted, the extended family you dreamed of, the tight-knit family unit you envisioned, and the safe, secure home you needed.

Admit that your life turned out differently from what you imagined it would and that you're disappointed, hurt, and angry about growing up in a dysfunctional family. If you are not able to do these things just yet, that's OK. Give yourself the freedom to work through your grief at your own pace.

What, specifically, do you need to grieve?

What step do you need to take to begin grieving that loss? Will you begin that process now? Explain.

Strengthening Your Roots

1. Think through the five stages of grief. When was a recent time you were stuck in one of the five stages of grief? We often struggle through the same stage repeatedly. In what ways do you have difficulty with this stage?

2. How can you use the power of God's Word and the Holy Spirit to work through that stage and toward the acceptance stage?

3. What things do you grieve not having in your reality childhood? How has this chapter helped you grieve the losses you experienced in your reality?

FEEDING YOUR FAITH

Learning the Skills to Cope

When we grieve, we often find ways of coping with our heavy emotions. Some people pray, others go for a jog, and some journal or talk it out with a friend or spouse. I teach yoga, which keeps me flexible, literally and figuratively. It keeps me balanced, giving me one hour of peace and quiet (a rare thing for a mother of five). And it helps me deal with stress and anxiety. Yoga also helps me win when I play Twister with my kids.

In my darkest days, however, I coped with stress and grief by over-exercising, restricting my diet, withdrawing from everyone around me, and indulging in other poisonous pursuits. Chances are, if you grew up in a dysfunctional family, you never learned healthy ways to handle anxiety either.

Martha Kate ❀ My eating disorder was my way of coping with what was happening around me. I took control of my body when I felt out of control with people, and it made me feel safe in the midst of the storm. Only after years of counseling did I realize why it was so hard to begin recovering from my eating disorder; I had used it to deal with the feelings and emotions in my family that I didn't want to face since I was ten years old.

Unhealthy Coping Skills

Before we consider emotionally and spiritually beneficial ways of handling our stress and grief, let's take a moment to consider unhealthy coping mechanisms (many in the form of addictions) we should avoid:

- Binge cleaning or organizing
- Compulsive spending, binge shopping, going into debt, living beyond our means
- Disordered eating, which describes any disturbed and unhealthy eating pattern:
  Anorexia
  Basing self-worth on body shape and weight
  Binge eating
  Bulimia
  Extremes of dieting
  Misuse of laxatives or diuretics
  Obsessive calorie counting
  Self-induced vomiting
  Skipping meals regularly
- Abusing alcohol or drugs (prescription or illegal)
- Fading into depression, which can include the following:[1]
  Becoming more irritable, short-tempered, or aggressive than usual
  Being unable to control negative thoughts
  Being unable to concentrate
  Changing sleep patterns and appetite
  Consuming more alcohol than usual or engaging in other reckless behavior
  Feeling hopeless and helpless
  Losing interest in activities, hobbies, and things you used to enjoy
- Gambling
- Gossiping
- Overexercising (also called exercise bulimia)
- Overserving in church or trying to look spiritual

- Raging
- Engaging in self-abuse
- Sleeping too much or too little
- Spending an excessive amount of time on social media
- Withdrawing from family and friends
- Withdrawing from God
- Working too much

Reread the list above, and then take a few minutes to engage in the exercise that follows.

1. Write a P next to each coping mechanism you saw your parents practice while you were growing up.

2. Write an S next to each coping mechanism you saw your siblings practice while you were growing up.

3. Write a G next to each coping mechanism you practiced while you were growing up.

4. Write an A next to each coping mechanism you currently practice as an adult.

5. Finally, write SO next to any of the behaviors you see in your significant other's life.

Now glance back at the list. Identify the behaviors that your parents or siblings engaged in that you see in yourself now that you are an adult.

Which unhealthy coping skills do both you and your significant other share?

What do these observations tell you?

Healthy Coping Skills

No one knows the cruel suffering of this world better than Jesus does, which is why He promises us, "In this world you will have trouble. But take heart! I have overcome the world" (John 16:33). Yes, we will have trials in this world. We will get laid off from work and lose our homes to foreclosure. We will raise children with special needs. We will give birth to stillborn babies. We will watch our parents die from cancer. We will wake up next to a spouse who feels like a stranger. And after surviving all this and more, we will wonder if we can make it . . . one . . . more . . . day.

The good news is this: we can, and we will. Our faithful, loving God assures us we can, saying, "So do not fear, for I am with you; do not be dismayed, for I am your God. I will strengthen you and help you; I will uphold you with my righteous right hand" (Isa. 41:10).

Fortunately, there are many life-giving, healthy coping skills we can use to work through our painful past, such as these:

- *Read Scripture.* The Bible isn't an instruction manual. It's God's words written specifically for us so that we can know Him personally. If we are not rooted in God's truth, nothing we do will move us from wounded to healing, because we will be acting out of our own strength instead of relying on the great Physician.
- *Pray.* Pour your heart out to God. Then pause long enough for God to respond.
- *Just say no.* Eliminate the activities and people that cause triggers. When you experience a trigger, write down what happened immediately preceding it, so you can avoid that situation in the future.

    Lighten your load by saying no to activities that clog up your schedule. Prioritize what is important to you and be prepared to disappoint people.
- *Rely on a supportive friend.* Friends often want to help, they just don't know how. Call someone who will listen when you need to talk.
- *Seek counseling.* I am a huge believer in seeking out pastoral and professional Christian counselors to help us grieve our past, engage

in our present, and empower us in our future. As we invest in and claim victory over our emotional and mental affliction, we will experience restoration. At the same time, we will remove the stigma from counseling and therapy—for ourselves and for others.

- *Take advantage of community resources.* Adam had Eve. Moses had Aaron. Naomi had Ruth. Jesus had the twelve disciples. Clearly, we were not meant to walk this road alone. God knows His people need each other to work through the messiness of life. That is why Solomon writes, "By yourself you're unprotected. With a friend you can face the worst. Can you round up a third? A three-stranded rope isn't easily snapped" (Eccl. 4:12 MSG).

    Many communities offer group recovery programs and other resources, such as Alcoholics Anonymous, Al Anon, Celebrate Recovery, DivorceCare, DC4Kids, Dealing with Divorce (for teens), and GriefShare.

- *Investigate prescription medication.* We live in a world that is trying to convince us that diet, exercise, oils, protein shakes, and juice fasts can cure all our ailments. While I believe these things can benefit some people, I also believe in the advantages of prescription medication. If you need medication, believe me when I say this: It's OK. You are not a failure. You are not weak. You are human.

The Truth About Depression

I struggled with depression after the birth of our third child, and when I did, I felt weak and ashamed. After grieving my feelings of failure, I felt God telling me, "Elizabeth, there is no shame in this. The shame is in suffering needlessly. The shame is in not being the mom your children deserve or the wife your husband desires because you refuse to seek the help you know is available."

I knew that day that I needed to let go of my pride. I called my doctor, and he prescribed the medication I needed. Slowly my depression lifted. One by one, I confided in a few close friends and realized I wasn't alone. Many of my friends had silently suffered too, just as embarrassed and ashamed as I was. My guess is that, with more than three hundred million people suffering from depression,[2] we all know someone in our community who is struggling—maybe that someone is you.

Maybe you are experiencing depression but think you have nothing to be depressed about. Your trauma occurred in childhood, and here you are, a fully functioning adult. You have a good job, great friends, an adoring husband, and a supportive church family. Nothing is particularly wrong with your life at this moment, so you wonder, *Why do I cry all the time? Why do I lash out? Why does life feel so hopeless?*

I felt the same way until my counselor brought to light a truth I had never considered. She said that as a child I considered trauma to be normal life stress. And as an adult, I didn't know how to process my current life stress, so I was responding the same way I had as a child; I was holding it together on the outside while I crumbled on the inside.

Through personal counseling and research I learned that depression, anxiety, hopelessness, and despair in our adult years may have nothing to do with our present and everything to do with our past. If you grew up in a dysfunctional family but never unpacked your baggage, this might be your body's way of telling you it is time to address your childhood.

Consider the following information reported by one survey:

- Women abused as children report more symptoms of depression, anxiety, low self-esteem, and substance abuse than women without a history of abuse.[3]
- These women are also at an increased risk for suicide, and that risk increases in proportion to the number of traumatic events she suffered as a child.[4]
- Childhood neglect and abuse are associated with increased risk for cardiac disease, peptic ulcers, autoimmune disease, diabetes, lung disease, and arthritic disorders.[5]
- "Women with a history of childhood abuse are more than twice as likely to develop depression as non-abused women."[6]
- "Childhood abuse is related to the development of anxiety disorders in adulthood."[7]

- "Childhood physical abuse predisposes for combat-related post-traumatic stress disorder (PTSD)."[8]
- Women abused before age thirteen are equally at risk for developing PTSD or major depressive disorder (MDD). Women abused after age thirteen are more likely to develop PTSD.[9]

Prescription medication, professional counseling, support groups, and mentors (which we will explain further in chapter 15) are all helpful resources to get you on the road to emotional, mental, physical, and spiritual recovery.

What healthy coping skills would you like to incorporate into your life?

Natalie ❀ I often withdraw. In my younger years, withdrawing was more of an unhealthy escape. I would hide away, sleep, and avoid everyone and everything, hoping that my reality would be different when I reemerged. As I've gotten older, I still tend to withdraw, but now I use that coping skill in a healthier way. I withdraw with better intent. I'm intentional about recognizing the pain that's causing my danger meter to register "Run now!" I'm intentional about laying that pain before Jesus. I'm intentional about spending quiet solitude with my Savior and His Word.

Relying on God as We Cope

I moved to a new town in the middle of my seventh-grade year, which is (in my opinion) the worst possible time to move. I thought I was cool, but my fellow students disagreed. Through hallway heckling, classroom pranks, and lunch-table rejection, they let me know that I was awkward, dorky, and dressed like a mom. It took me awhile to adjust to the social hierarchy and wardrobe expectations in a small Texas town, but I laid low, read lots of fashion tips in *Teen Magazine* (life before Pinterest), and eventually upped my cool factor. By high school I was no longer a social disaster. In fact, I had a great group of friends, was involved in sports and other activities, and made good grades.

As I mentioned in the previous chapter, life at home was stormy. So I did what most kids from dysfunctional families do—I found a way to cope. I created a "perfect" world for myself at school. It became a place of refuge, stability, and safety. Friends became family—#framily.

Author Mark Harris writes, "Coming out of the brokenness of their own family many [Generation] Xer's place a high value on friendship and community. Friends are the bottom line value of this generation."[10] Harris is right. When families fail us we turn to friends to fill the void.

After my mom's second divorce, we moved to a new city. I was devastated. I didn't know how I was going to cope with losing my community, my activities, my framily—the entire identity I had created.

While relying on my newfound faith to sustain me through this difficult time, I stumbled upon the following verse, "With man this is impossible, but with God all things are possible" (Matt. 19:26).

I knew God was speaking to me: *Elizabeth, you will never get through this on your own. Don't turn to your friends, and don't run away from me. I am here with you. I love you. I will get you through this. Overcoming your problems by relying on others and yourself is impossible. But if you rely on me, all things are possible.*

The hashtag #framily is popular for a reason; people are growing deeper roots with their friends than they are with their families. Framily can be both a positive and a negative presence in our lives. How has your framily helped you cope with the dysfunction in your family of origin?

How has your framily served as a place of escape and allowed you to ignore issues you need to deal with in your family of origin?

Strengthening Your Roots

1. Take a few moments to go back and read through the list of unhealthy coping skills. Are there any that you use in your life to escape the pain of your reality? If so, list them here:

How can you use this information to move forward in a positive way?

2. Look back at the list of healthy coping skills. Which ones are you using to help you deal with your current stresses and grief?

3. How did you cope with your dysfunctional family while growing up?

In what ways did this help you survive turmoil at home?

In what ways did it make things worse?

THE MASTER GARDENER
Discovering God's Role

After my mom's second divorce, she dragged me to church—against my will. I went, kicking and screaming. It proved to be the best thing she ever did for me.

As a straight-A student in school, I snubbed the church. I felt forced to don a scarlet F on my chest there, because I didn't know the Bible stories or where to look up certain verses. I owned a Bible for the first time in my life as a high school freshman, but I couldn't make any sense of the passages. And honestly, the youth group kids jamming out to Michael W. Smith and Amy Grant were too cheesy for me. (If I ever meet Michael or Amy, my apologies in advance.)

Week after week my mom insisted I go, so I trudged along. And week after week I heard the gospel that slowly melted away my pride. I heard the preacher talk about Jesus, the cross, and the resurrection. This was not the dream I had envisioned. Nor was it the harsh reality I had known for so long. This was the life-changing gospel. I felt it in my soul.

At fifteen years old, I walked down the aisle to the front of the church (very old-school Southern Baptist style) and accepted Jesus as my Savior on Easter Sunday.

Natalie ✳ I am most grateful to my parents for always pointing me back to Jesus. They never wavered in their faith. Their faith was and is very real to them, and I've followed their model and tried to emulate them in my family.

However, after some time and counseling, I have realized that their faith included self-righteousness and works-based love, which isn't the way of Jesus. It was part of our religion as I was growing up, but it's definitely not the way of Jesus.

What role did religion, Scripture, or church play in your family of origin?

How did turmoil push you toward or away from knowing Jesus as your Savior?

If you can, identify the point at which you knew the reality of Jesus as your Savior. Supply as many details as you can.

Finding God in the Best Parts and Worst Parts

Fast-forward into my twenties. Determined to shed my F-student self-image in respect to Bible knowledge, I enrolled in seminary. One of my professors asked us to make a timeline of our lives. He called it our "Stars and Scars," meaning the highs and lows in our lives. After we created the timelines, he asked us to describe how God had played a role in these moments in our lives. The thing I found most interesting was that God showed up more in my scars than in my stars.

My husband, Brandon, and I have instated a nightly dinner table tradition in our family, in which we share the best part of our day and the worst part of our day. We call it "Best Part/Worst Part." For our kids, the best part of their day is always "school."

"Elaborate please. Math tests and recess cannot both be your best part."

For the worst part they often say, "nothing." You might think their response would make this mama happy. But it doesn't. *Something* has to be the worst part. *Everything* can't be the best part. Just keeping it real, people.

I want them to have a worst part of the day because it is in the worst parts of life, when we feel withered and worn like a crunched up leaf lying on the ground getting stepped on over and over again, that we learn something. We learn very little, if anything, from Ice Cream Day in the cafeteria (except that drumsticks rock and popsicles are lame) or from playing dodgeball (best game ever).

When our best friend refuses to play with us, we learn what it means to feel lonely, and without having felt loneliness, we might never have the compassion to invite the new kid to sit with us at lunch. When we fail a spelling test, we develop a stronger work ethic, and without failure, we might feel entitled to that big promotion.

I don't want my children's lives to be filled with suffering. But I do want their lives to be filled with Jesus. And a little heartache may be the catalyst that pushes them toward their Savior. Loneliness, shame, emptiness, and disappointment can direct us to the one true God who can fill us up.

Think right now about a painful childhood memory (a scar). What did you feel at the time?

What did you learn from that experience?

Would you have learned that lesson any other way?

How long after feeling the pain did you discover God's role in the situation?

How did this experience shape your faith?

Naomi and Ruth

My daughter Clarey was six years old when she and I read through the book of Ruth together. It easily held her attention because it contains the secret recipe all girls enjoy: *drama!* Right in the first five verses Naomi leaves her family, friends, and culture and relocates to a new town completely devoid of people who share her faith. She gains two daughters-in-law but loses her husband and two sons. The three women have no way to earn money so that they can eat or live. I'm barely into the story, and I'm already emotionally spent.

When Naomi accepts that the ideal future she envisioned—growing old with her husband, surrounded by her children and grandchildren—is gone, she becomes bitter. "'Don't call me Naomi,' she told them. 'Call me Mara, because the Almighty has made my life very bitter. I went away full, but the Lord has brought me back empty'" (Ruth 1:20–21). That's drama. If I were Ruth, I would pull Naomi aside and say, "Excuse me? Empty? I'm standing *right here!*"

Despite Naomi's lack of faith, God does not forsake her. In fact, quite the opposite occurs. At every turn in the story, we see God pursuing Naomi, eager to show her that He has plans to give new life to her dying family tree.

Read each of the verses below, and then write a brief summary of how God pursues Naomi and shows her favor. (The book of Ruth is only four chapters, so if you would rather read the entire book, more power to you, sister!)

- Ruth 1:8–18

- Ruth 2:8–20

- Ruth 3:1–6, 10–13

- Ruth 4:2–10

- Ruth 4:17–22

Time and again God pursues His daughter, Naomi. When her family tree withers, she becomes bitter, lonely, and hopeless. (Even Naomi experienced various stages of grief.) But little by little she regains hope. She realizes that God is for her, not against her. And I want you to know that He is for you too. That is why He sent His Son, Jesus Christ, to earth to die on the cross for us—which makes this gospel far better than any dream you could imagine.

Jesus's Role in Your Story

If you spent years daydreaming about a happy ending, chances are yours was one where the guy gets the girl, the lost is found, and the good triumphs over the evil. But in your reality, the Enemy has been hard at work lying, tempting, and deceiving everyone around you. And he's very good at it. Because of Satan's evil scheming, there's always tension between the life we dream about and the reality we actually live out, so let me offer you reasons to focus on the gospel, a more reliable, sustainable lens through which you can view life.

1. *The gospel is a true story about a God who saves people.* Only one hero exists and He is Jesus Christ—the Great Rescuer. He brings freedom, peace, and comfort to those who want a relationship with Him.

2. *The gospel requires that we let go of our childhood fantasies.* We must accept the pain of our past and the reality of our present, and deal with the consequences of both, so we can experience true restoration. This is why the previous chapters of this book are so important. We must work through past memories, unpack and discard our baggage, and then develop healthy coping skills, so we can release the pipe dreams we've conjured up in our minds. Only then can we embrace the gospel God offers us.

3. *The gospel asks us to embrace more than shallow spirituality.* Jesus is our living, breathing God who walks among His people, heals the sick, sits with children, loves the unwanted, forgives the sinners, and offers light to a dark world. Our culture, however, likes to water down faith; reduce prayer to moments of silence; and sport WWJD bumper stickers, bracelets, and T-shirts, as long as they don't offend anyone or require actual life change. Accordingly, we tend to forget that Jesus is fully God and fully man—the Word made flesh. He is the way and the truth and the life.

4. *The gospel is the point at which Jesus interjects Himself into our lives.* What He is doing is not always apparent on the surface, but God is working behind the scenes—and His story is always worth waiting to hear. When it is finally known, God's story will be more dynamic than our grandest dreams, and it will be full of ways in which God used us for His glory.

Take time now to journal the ways in which God has walked with you through your journey. Use the following questions to help you get started.

In what ways were you protected over the years from unhealthy people or situations?

When did things work in your favor even when it seemed as if the odds were against you?

How has God taken something the Enemy meant for evil and turned it into something for your good?

Where did you find genuine comfort and safety in some of your most desperate, painful moments?

The beauty of releasing your daydreams, grieving your lost childhood, and embracing the gospel is that, through it all, you will encounter your one true Savior. He has been with you the entire time, waiting for you to feel His presence and longing for you to recognize His love. He has been actively involved in your life, even when it felt as if He were absent. While it might seem like a journey full of uncertainty, embracing the gospel is always worthwhile. I think even your childhood self, the part of you longing for a happy ending, would agree.

Strengthening Your Roots

1. Do you agree with me that we learn more from our worst parts, or scars, than from our best parts, or stars? Explain.

2. Think about a few of your best parts from your growing up years. What life lessons did you learn?

How did each of those lessons influence your relationship with God?

3. Now think about a few of your worst parts from your growing up years. What life lessons did you learn?

How did each of those lessons influence your relationship with God?

4. Have you released your idyllic dream, grieved your lost childhood, and embraced the gospel? If so, how has it affected your life? If not, what is holding you back from doing so?

If you have not embraced the gospel, I encourage you to get together with a friend, a mentor, a pastor, or someone else you trust. Let them know your end goal is to move in this direction and that you need prayer and a friend to walk with you in this journey.

PART TWO

THE PRESENT

THE GARDEN GATE
Learning the Importance of Boundaries

We love our dog, Marley (except when she eats socks and runs up our vet bill). Marley is a Wheaten Terrier–Poodle, a "whoodle" in the dog world. She is a lot like our children: wiry and high-energy, young and agile, intelligent and in need of boundaries. She needs a fence to keep her off the road so she doesn't get hit by a car. (She also needs a kennel to sleep in so she won't roam around the house and use the carpet as a toilet—don't ask!)

Many of us have people in our lives who, much like Marley, need fences—or boundaries—for a number of reasons:

- To create clear expectations
- To keep our relationship in a peaceful place
- To protect our own emotional and mental health and the emotional and mental health of our spouse and children
- To maintain our physical safety and the physical safety of our spouse and children
- To create an atmosphere of stability in our home and family
- To protect ourselves against the dysfunctional atmosphere of our family of origin
- To teach our family of origin how we want to be treated

In the list above, place a check mark next to the reasons that explain why you need to draw healthy boundaries with your family of origin.

Discovering the Reasons Behind Boundaries

If your family of origin lacked boundaries, you might recognize some of these characteristics in your family members or in yourself:[1]

- A desire for instant gratification
- A pull toward irresponsible or toxic people and the desire to fix them
- A victim mentality
- A tendency toward addiction and compulsive behavior
- An inability to resolve conflict constructively
- An inability to respect personal space
- An inability to say no
- An inability to set limits
- Difficulty maintaining intimacy and close relationships with others
- Disorganization
- A lack of follow-through
- A tendency toward oversharing or undersharing
- An inability to relate to one's family (otherwise known as "detached")
- An inability to respect another person's feelings or position in a relationship
- A tendency to dominate in a relationship
- An inability to separate from one's family (otherwise known as "enmeshed")
- An unwillingness to compromise
- A lack of privacy
- A tendency to become promiscuous
- A tendency to feel guilt for setting and enforcing boundaries later in life

In the above list, checkmark the characteristics that describe your family of origin. Then circle the ones that describe you.

The apostle Paul writes, "For God is not a God of disorder but of peace—as in all the congregations of the Lord's people" (1 Cor. 14:33). Boundaries bring peace, order, and security to the chaos that ensues in families. Other benefits, such as the following, flow from drawing healthy boundaries:

1. They create clear expectations.
2. They teach people how to treat us.
3. They protect us emotionally, spiritually, mentally, and physically.
4. They empower us and help us meet our own needs.

Learning How to Draw Healthy Boundaries

Since 2007, Brandon and I have led groups of engaged couples through premarital education classes. We love their giddy demeanor and their sweet outlook on the future. We also enjoy teaching them the wisdom we've accrued through mistakes we've made over the years.

One such mistake occurred when we were engaged. My mom had remarried again, and Brandon and I had gone to visit her and my stepdad for the weekend. I'll let Brandon tell the rest of the story in his own words.

"We were staying at Elizabeth's mom and stepdad's house for the weekend, and we were all getting ready to go to a big family event. Everyone was busy getting dressed, fixing hair, and hurrying around. I don't know why, but there was a lot of tension in the air. For some reason that tension was unnecessarily taken out on Elizabeth. I stood there, paralyzed with shock and fear. I had never seen anyone treat their daughter like that. I didn't know my place, so I followed Elizabeth's lead. She said nothing (which I later discovered was because she had spent a lifetime saying nothing). I took her silence as permission for me to say nothing. However, in hindsight I realized that I had failed to protect my fiancée. I missed the chance to draw boundaries with my future in-laws. And that day was the beginning of a lot of damage we had to undo later."

Yes, all married couples must learn to draw healthy boundaries with their families, and for adults who come from broken branches, this practice proves even more crucial, but challenging.

Learning how to draw healthy boundaries with your family of origin so you can create a restored, vital, godly family of your own is a delicate process with two main requisites: *empathy*—understanding your family of origin—and *respect*—appropriately honoring your parents.

Understanding Leads to Empathy

In my junior year of high school my English teacher assigned the book *A Yellow Raft in Blue Water*. The book tells the tale of three generations of women: Rayona, a half-Native American teenage girl; her mother, Christine; and Christine's mom, Ida (who is actually not Christine's birth mom but her half sister and cousin, as we later find out). Talk about broken branches! For half the time I was reading, I felt as if I were tuning in to an episode of *Jerry Springer*.

The author divides the book into three sections, each part told from a different woman's point of view. As I read the first part of the book, told from Rayona's point of view, I found myself angry with Christine, whose reckless self-centeredness drove her to choose her own desires over the welfare of her daughter—every single time. Rayona says about her mother, Christine, "She lights Kent after Kent and the room fills with smoke while she kills the bottle. . . . Those nights I help her to bed."[2]

But when the narrative switched to Christine's point of view, I suddenly found myself empathizing with her. A peek into her childhood helped me understand Christine at her core as a lonely, regretful, sad woman who is searching for love.

While I gained empathy for Christine, I began to judge Ida who took Christine in as her own child when Christine was a baby. As a mother, I find it difficult to understand why Ida volunteered to raise Christine only to spend a lifetime rejecting her.

Maybe you recognize this in the context of your own family of origin. Understanding your parents' past could lead you to a place of empathy. If you approach them with empathy, you can create emotional and practical boundaries that are not spiteful but healthy and productive for you, your marriage, and your parents.

Martha Kate ❀ The more my adult relationship develops with my parents, the more I understand and empathize with them. I truly believe that they were doing the best they could my entire childhood. When I look at it that way, I am able to forgive them for certain situations that developed during my childhood. My parents now accept responsibility, and they understand that how they were raised made them who they were as parents with young children. While their best wasn't always what was good or healthy for me, I do believe that they were trying their best. By the grace of God, I now have a healthy relationship with my parents. That transformation has so much more to do with God changing my heart than it does with my ability to understand, empathize, and forgive.

Remembering Memories Differently

By reading the same memories from different points of view in *A Yellow Raft in Blue Water*, I learned that two or more people can live through the same experience and remember it in completely different ways. This happens for various reasons.

- Different people might *perceive* an event differently at the time it originally occurs. Hypothetically, your dad missed your high school graduation because he thought you said it was at three o'clock when you really said twelve thirty. He brushed it off as a simple case of miscommunication—no big deal. You felt it was a classic example of his self-centeredness, of his failure to listen to you and make you a priority.
- One person *reminisces* about the memory more than the other person. Returning to our hypothetical example, because your dad missed your high school graduation, you felt deeply wounded, and you replayed the event in your mind over and over again. Your dad, however, apologized, gave you a graduation gift of a thousand dollars, and moved on. He thought he had made amends. Little

did he know you didn't want his money; you wanted his time. You didn't want him to apologize; you wanted him to change. Repeating the event in your mind solidifies the memory in your brain, and ten years later you remember it vividly, but your dad barely remembers it at all.

- One person's *feelings* at the time of the event influence the memory of the incident.[3] If you were already hurt by your dad before he missed your graduation, that monumental event confirmed what you already suspected—your dad loves himself more than he loves you. When he continues his behavior pattern of making promises but rarely delivering, you become hard-hearted toward him. Those calloused feelings cloud your memory and make graduation day even more painful than it was the day it occurred.
- A person's *intellectual and emotional maturity* influence their perceptions of reality differently. When your dad missed your high school graduation, he hurt you deeply. If, however, your dad missed your law school graduation when you were thirty-five years old, you might not have felt so wounded and therefore would not have dwelt on the issue for so long.

If you perceive the same memory in a different way from your parents, you have several healthy options for responding:

- Write them a letter.
- Talk to them about the situation.
- Quietly extend forgiveness in your heart but never reach out.
- Offer them forgiveness and begin rebuilding your relationship.
- Offer them forgiveness and begin rebuilding your relationship while incorporating healthy boundaries.

As issues and memories surface, I encourage you to pray first, seek the Lord's leading, and then proceed out of obedience. Remember, God sent Jesus to earth to reconcile God's people to Him, and God longs for His people to achieve reconciliation with one another as well. He doesn't want our branches to stay broken and decayed but to gain strength and vitality as we come together in His name.

> "If it is possible, as far as it depends on you, live at peace with everyone" (Rom. 12:18).

Showing Respect and Honor

We read the commandment to honor our fathers and mothers twice in the Old Testament (Exod. 20:12; Lev. 19:3). For many people, however, the requirement to honor someone who violated, abandoned, degraded, controlled, disrespected, or ignored them might drive them away from the church and away from God altogether.

The key to being able to honor our parents is setting emotion aside and remembering the natural order God created. Just as marriage is a representation of Christ and the church, parents and children represent God and His people. Whether we honor our parents is an ongoing choice. According to Dr. John Constable, professor at Dallas Theological Seminary, "The Israelites were to honor God because He had given them life, and they were to honor their parents because they were [God's] instruments in giving them life."[4] If you can find no other reason to honor your parents, you can honor them simply because they gave you life and breath.

Many people don't know how to honor their parents practically, so let me offer some simple suggestions to get you started:

- *Start small.* Respect doesn't always come in the form of grand gestures, but can be displayed through birthday cards, Mother's Day and Father's Day cards, and other notes. Assuming they are not a danger to you or your children, offer to meet them for a casual lunch or coffee or invite them to your child's birthday party. Reaching out to them in small ways can effectively show them honor.
- *Respect them in your speech and interactions.* Be careful how you

talk to and about your family of origin around your friends and children. Even if you're wrestling with negative feelings, strive to honor your parents around other people.

- *Forgive them.* I know, that's easier said than done. But you can start the forgiveness process by asking God to move your heart in this direction. Then search your heart; ask God to show you any offenses for which you need to be forgiven. Forgiveness does not mean always bending to their will. (More on this in chapter 14.)
- *Pray for them.* Pray for their salvation and their journey of restoration. Also, pray for yourself, that you would see your family through a lens of compassion and love.

Maintaining Boundaries

While we want to empathize with and respect our parents, we still need to draw and maintain healthy boundaries if our parents or their environment are toxic. Unfortunately, many of us who grew up in dysfunctional families might not know the practical steps to take to ensure our mental, emotional, physical, and spiritual health.

Here is a list to get you started:

1. *Release false hope.* Let go of the hope that someday things will change: "Someday they will love me." "Someday my family will look the way I dreamed." Accept the life you knew growing up so you can become emotionally available for the life God has given you.
2. *Accept the truth.* Accept that boundaries are not selfish but are actually a very loving way to respond to your family while getting your own needs met.
3. *Accept the risk.* When drawing boundaries, you must risk losing your parents' affection, approval, or your relationship with them. When controlling parents are suddenly told how they must treat someone, they often respond by retaliating. This step might require you to tell your mom that she cannot come to Thanksgiving dinner at your house if she is drunk. You might tell your dad that if he criticizes

your appearance, then you will no longer spend time with him. These difficult words are necessary if you want to change the way your parents treat you.

4. *Present a united front.* Agree with your spouse on the boundaries you plan to set, and present your boundaries as a decision you made together.

5. *Communicate your boundaries.* Decide whether you will communicate your boundaries directly to your family or just let them play out naturally.

Natalie ✳ I wrestle with honoring and respecting my parents but imposing boundaries. I'm not sure I'm doing it right. My husband and I fall very hard on the boundaries side, which tends to convey the message that we don't honor or respect them (at least from their perspective). I love my parents, and they love me—in their way. It's taken me a long time to realize that, but now I believe that they did the best they could. There are consequences to all our actions, however, and theirs have left us with a broken relationship.

Which of the five steps can you begin to implement and how?

Over the years I have mentored many women and young married couples who have said that it would be so much easier if their family just wasn't in their life. Maybe so, but God doesn't call us to an easy life; He calls us to a grace-filled life. Sometimes God keeps our families of origin—even if they are corrupt—in our life for a reason.

- So we can be a light in their lives
- So we can minister to them
- To refine us
- To make us depend on God for patience and strength

Strengthening Your Roots

1. Have you ever remembered an event differently than someone close to you remembered it? If so, why do you think your memories differed?

How did you feel when they told a different account? Invalidated? Angry? Hurt? Something else? Explain.

2. *A Yellow Raft in Blue Water* perfectly illustrates how digging deep into the roots of one's past brings understanding and empathy for family members. Write a paragraph summarizing your mom's childhood and teen years. Then do the same for your dad's childhood and teen years. (If you don't know about your parents' past, would you be willing to ask them or another family member in order to move toward forgiveness and healing? If not, what is holding you back?)

3. Now that you've reflected on your parents' past, what helps you understand their behavior—words and actions and choices—toward you when you were a child?

What helps you understand their thoughts, words, and actions toward you now that you are an adult?

4. Describe what it would look like for you to honor your father and mother.

In what areas do you have difficulty honoring your parents? What makes it difficult?

5. Have you set any healthy boundaries with your family of origin? If so, what are they? If not, what boundaries do you need to establish with your family of origin?

If you've not set boundaries, what's preventing you from doing so? Are you willing to make the commitment to begin setting those boundaries today?

7

A BEAUTIFUL ARRANGEMENT
Comparing Contracts and Covenants

When Brandon graduated from law school, we celebrated the day with a family party and a viewing of the newly released movie *Legally Blonde*, starring Reese Witherspoon. Brandon confirmed that law school was exactly as Reese portrayed it (insert eye roll), and I confirmed that "whoever said orange is the new pink is seriously disturbed." Brandon had worked hard for his new career, and I was excited for the journey that lay before him.

Fast-forward a couple of years. We sat at the dinner table while Brandon described one of his cases. "I don't understand," I said, appalled at the injustice. "It sounds like the details are spelled out in the contract. How can the other party escape their responsibility?"

"People break contracts every day," Brandon said casually, already calloused after only a short time on the job. "Contracts were made to be broken. That's why I have a job."

That began our ongoing discussion of contracts versus covenants as it applies to our own marriage as well as to the relationships of the engaged and young married couples we mentor. A contract is much like a little potted plant our preschooler brought home from school one day. It was cute and sweet and meant to teach him about plants, but it wasn't meant to remain viable indefinitely. A covenant, however, is like a strong oak planted one hundred years ago. It has history, fortitude, beauty, and purpose. It is meant to stand the test of time.

If you and I want to strengthen our families' roots and watch strong branches grow for generations to come, we need to plant strong oaks, not tiny potted plants. We need to understand both the obvious and the more subtle differences between contracts and covenants and how these differences affect our marriages.

The Marriage Contract

Several requirements exist for an agreement to be considered a contract:

- It legally binds two or more parties.
- It states what the parties will do or will not do or both.
- It is written down.
- It is enforceable by law. (Of course, as my attorney husband likes to point out, it is often neither binding nor enforceable. Ugh.)

Our culture, including Christian culture, has watered down the marriage covenant (which we will discuss in a moment) into a less binding contract for the sake of convenience. We often believe our friends, family, the media, and sometimes even the church when they convey these deceptions:

- Marriage is designed to serve our ever-changing needs.
- God wants us to be happy at all costs.
- If we follow Jesus, we deserve health, wealth, and happiness.
- Marriage isn't for forever; it's for right now.

The Barna Group conducts in-depth research on marriage and divorce, among many other topics. They recently reported that, among Christian and non-Christian Americans, "there no longer seems to be much of a stigma attached to divorce; it is now seen as an unavoidable rite of passage."[1]

The research even indicated that many young people embrace the idea of serial marriage, where first marriages are trial runs, allowing couples to figure out life, love, and themselves. So while we take pride in claiming that America is the most evolved, the most progressive, the most elite nation in the world, our lack of commitment to marriage, even as Christians, says otherwise.

It seems attorneys aren't the only ones complacent about our right to break a legal contract. But God knows marriage doesn't fall under the same umbrella as a rental agreement or a medical procedure gone awry—which is why He never intended for marriage to be a contract. So let's take a look at what God did intend for marriage.

The Marriage Covenant

I admit that most of my wedding ceremony is a pretty hazy memory. I don't remember a lot, but I do remember two things. At the end of the ceremony our pastor turned Brandon and me around to face our friends and family, and he said, "Never again will you see all these people gathered in one room to support you." That stuck with me because I had never grown up with much community. We had moved around so much, bouncing from place to place and school to school, that we didn't have deeply planted roots, yet there sat a chapel full of people, gathered to tell us they believed in us; they supported our union; and they looked forward to watching us journey through life together.

Then he said, "What therefore God hath joined together, let not man put asunder" (Mark 10:9 KJV). Now, I'm usually not one for ol' King James. It's a bit stuffy and old school, and it makes me feel as if I should be drinking tea with my pinky raised. But in this case, I melted. After years of living through divorces, abandonment, chaos, and unrest, these words sounded beautiful and peaceful, as if God were wrapping Brandon and me in a warm blanket, holding us close, and saying, "I will never let you go." This was our marriage covenant.

What are your hopes for your own marriage covenant?

A marriage covenant is much like a contract. Both are binding agreements, which state what the parties will and will not do; in marriage we call these wedding vows (we will love, honor, cherish, etc.). Both marriage covenants and contracts are written—this is why we obtain our wedding license and sign it on our wedding day. Finally, a marriage covenant is enforceable by law, which is why it takes only a few minutes to get married (hello, Las Vegas wedding chapels) and many months, if not years, to get divorced.

However, a marriage covenant differs from a contract in two important ways. First, contracts have loopholes because they are based on both parties fulfilling expectations. Thus, contracts were made to be broken. Marriage, however, is not meant to last for only a limited time. God intends marriage to last for a lifetime.

> Jesus said, "Moses wrote this command only as a concession to your hardhearted ways. In the original creation, God made male and female to be together. Because of this, a man leaves father and mother, and in marriage he becomes one flesh with a woman—no longer two individuals, but forming a new unity. Because God created this organic union of the two sexes, no one should desecrate his art by cutting them apart." (Mark 10:5–9 msg)

In contrast to our cultural mentality, which is ruled by a self-serving focus, the marriage covenant is ruled by an others-first mind-set. If we want a healthy marriage, we must serve our partners. We must offer our spouses enjoyable sex as well as great conversation. We must be willing to discuss finances as well as go on date nights. Marriage is all-encompassing and complex. It is not a pie out of which we choose the pieces we want to eat, allowing the remainder to mold on the kitchen counter. We must engage in things that are important to our spouse, even if they are not high on our own priority list. "Do nothing out of selfish ambition or vain conceit. Rather, in humility value others above yourselves, not looking to your own interests but each of you to the interests of the others" (Phil. 2:3–4).

Elyse ❋ I wish someone would have told me that saying yes to a marriage proposal means saying yes to never trying to change the proposer. When you agree to marriage, you agree to take on a husband's issues and shortcomings, not to save him. And you cannot make a man change simply by believing in him enough. Rescue, change, and conviction are reserved for the Holy Spirit. When the Holy Spirit does change your spouse, that change will directly change you also. On the flip side, one's own refusal to be led by the Spirit—rescued, changed, and convicted by the Spirit—will directly affect your partner. Entering a covenant and becoming one flesh has severe consequences for each person—both good and bad.

Throughout the Bible we see God make covenants with His people: the Noahic covenant in which God sent a rainbow and promised to never again flood the earth; the Abrahamic covenant in which God promised to give Abraham many descendants; and the Mosaic covenant in which God gave Moses His divine law and promised to set Israel apart from the rest of the people.

As you can see, God created covenants for the benefit of His kingdom and to bless His people. The same is true of the marriage covenant. Our marriages always exist to serve God's kingdom, and they always strengthen us.

A covenant is also based on steadfast, unconditional love. Since Brandon and I got married, we have navigated chronic illness, loss of a parent, relocating, serving in the community, job changes, unexpected pregnancy, finances, children's health issues, depression, starting a nonprofit, unmet expectations, foster care, adoption, remodeling a house, and navigating ministry. All these things require time and emotional energy. We know we would not be able to juggle the stress of life without a strong, unwavering love founded in Christ.

Karen ✹ Marriage is not about feelings; it's about covenant, commitment, servanthood, and becoming more Christlike.

Let me take a moment to address those of you who have a husband who does not love you with a pure heart. He may have loved you once, but now he only likes you sometimes. He may not know how to love you, or perhaps he loves what you can offer him. He looks out for himself. He doesn't support your dreams. He doesn't encourage your interests. Maybe you married him hoping he would change; if you offered enough patience, kindness, loyalty, and love, then God would fix him. Friends, life is not a dreamy romantic comedy. Your significant other is not a fixer-upper. He is an adult and responsible for his own actions, and he's not fulfilling his covenantal responsibilities to you. (Bear in mind that some breaches of the marriage covenant—such as physical violence, infidelity, or abandonment—should be addressed with godly outside counsel and may require prayerful intervention.)

> *Leslie* ✸ I wish someone had told me that you won't always like your spouse but you can still love him.

Whether our husbands love and care for us as God intends, we are required to love and respect them (Eph. 5:33; John 13:34). Neither spouse is perfect, and we are all in need of our Savior. Accountability, forgiveness, and grace are biblically mandated. We must comply, all while relying on God for the strength we do not possess. "For if you forgive other people when they sin against you, your heavenly Father will also forgive you. But if you do not forgive others their sins, your Father will not forgive your sins" (Matt. 6:14–15).

The Benefits of Covenant Marriage

Increasing numbers of couples today are choosing to live together before marriage. Accepting premarital cohabitation as an option, unfortunately, has become more culturally acceptable. And culture, of course, seeps into the church.

Pamela J. Smock, director and research professor at the Population Studies Center at the University of Michigan, claimed that cohabitation has become "the new normal."[2] NBC News journalist Aleccia Jonel elaborates, "By the time they're 20, 1 in 4 women ages 15 to 44 in the U.S. have lived with a man, and by the time they're 30, that ratio climbs to 3 in 4."

You or someone you know may be one of the "one in four" or "three in four" women who has chosen to cohabit, and you don't think it's a big deal.

You're trying to save money and don't want to pay two rents. Or maybe your parents, siblings, or friends chose this route so cohabitation seems "normal." Whatever your thoughts on cohabitation, it's a choice to establish a household apart from marriage. Biblical covenant marriage is more than a wedding ceremony, guests, and a signed document. It's God's created design for His people. Here are a few reasons why it's such a sacred event:

1. *Covenant marriage brings security. Cohabitation brings questions.* Almost every book on dating, engagement, marriage, or sex delivers a loud and clear message that women need emotional, physical, and financial security. If you come from broken branches, chances are your home lacked security and stability, so your need probably intensified. A covenant marriage provides the security you crave; cohabitation fosters a get-out-quick mind-set.

2. *Covenant marriage provides commitment. Cohabitation leads to broken promises.* Living together can be like an endless slumber party. When reality hits—the bills are due, the other person's parents act controlling, or friends get annoying—either one of you can bail. It's easy to play house when you know you can always walk out the door. It's tough to commit. Cohabiting is a public statement that you're taking a test drive.

Franny ❀ Love is easy. Marriage is work.

3. *Covenant marriage assumes hardship. Cohabitation comes with an escape hatch.* Eternal butterflies are a myth, and if you're living together or believe that your marriage contract can be broken, you have an easy out once adversity enters your relationship and the butterflies stop fluttering.

Natalie ❀ I believed it would be different for my husband and me. Surely we would be the couple that always had butterflies. I thought we would always know and provide what the other person needed and that we would never cease to communicate effortlessly.

4. *Covenant marriage acknowledges human imperfection. Cohabitation assumes the ideal.* Our spouses will disappoint us, just as we will disappoint them. Covenant marriage forces us to face our humanity and work through our disenchantments, to hold on to the cross, and to extend grace and forgiveness when all we want to do is cling to our pride. Recognizing we are both human brings us closer to one another and forces us to rely on Jesus.

Ellie ✸ I wish I had known that my spouse would disappoint me, hurt me, and fail me and that I would do the same to him—not because we don't love or care for one another deeply, but because we are imperfect and sinful.

List three ways you show your humanness and how that causes tension in your marriage.

List three ways your spouse shows his humanness and how that causes tension in your marriage.

5. *Covenant marriage embraces disagreement. Cohabitation views disagreement as a potential threat.* Our backgrounds, expectations, preferences, and personalities all contribute to our decisions and choices, so it's no surprise we will eventually disagree. In a contract or cohabitation situation, disagreements breed fear because the outcome could lead to irreparable damage, rejection, and separation. However, in a covenant marriage disagreements are safe, welcomed, and encouraged because we can grow and learn from them.

I'm passionate about building covenant marriages. This passion isn't birthed through reading textbook cases or statistics. It comes from life experience. I want God's abundant life for you. Will you take it? Will you allow God to reclaim your family tree?

Strengthening Your Roots

1. Would you describe your family of origin as an example of a contract marriage or a covenant marriage? Explain.

2. Of the five benefits of covenant marriage, which one is most important to you? Explain.

3. God pours out sacrificial, steadfast love upon His children. He then gives us the opportunity to live out this same kind of love through the covenant of marriage. How have you seen that love playing out in your own marriage?

IN FULL BLOOM
Balancing Roles and Responsibilities

Most of my life I watched my single mom play the roles of mom, dad, and wife. While she juggled a lot to keep our little family together, I also endured a revolving door of boyfriends, as well as a couple of stepdads. This constant turnover taught me that roles in marriage are subjective, murky, and sometimes even chaotic.

So you can imagine my role confusion when I married Brandon. I thought that in order to make my marriage work I needed to do the opposite of what I saw growing up, which meant becoming the quintessential housewife—you know, the woman who cooks four-course meals every night, keeps the house immaculate, and makes her husband priority number one, while having no outside interests of her own. While this might work for some women, I was miserable. I knew I was living a lie.

On the outside, our newlywed life looked as if it were blossoming. On the inside, I felt like a lifeless twig. I didn't know how to play the role of a wife while retaining my identity. I didn't know how to balance working full-time, loving my husband, creating a welcoming home, maintaining my friendships, serving in my church, and accomplishing all the other things in my *Perfect Wife Handbook*.

One night, after a not-so-perfect-wife meltdown, Brandon and I had a heart-to-heart talk. "I don't need the table set and dinner cooked every night," he explained. "I was raised on Luby's Cafeteria for dinner three times a week." (And can you believe that after all the training I've given him over the years, this man still believes macaroni and cheese is a vegetable because it is in the vegetable section at Luby's? Ugh.)

We talked some more about wants, needs, and expectations. Brandon helped me realize that much of my frustration—OK, all of it—was due to unrealistic standards I'd placed on myself. Many women who come from dysfunctional or divorced families don't know how to love or serve their husbands well because they didn't have healthy role models. Instead of seeing humility, forgiveness, and laughter in our parents' marriages, we saw fighting, abandonment, fear, neglect, control, or tension.

We also may not understand the difference between roles and responsibilities—which was really my core issue. I didn't understand that every husband and wife has responsibilities, things that must be done in order to make the marriage function (little things like cooking dinner, taking out the trash, and washing the dishes). Fortunately, I have five children now—I've gotten really good at delegating my responsibilities.

I also did not understand that aside from mundane responsibilities, husbands and wives also have roles in the marriage. The world tries to tell us that a husband's role and a wife's role are equal and interchangeable. The Bible, however, tells us these roles are equal, yes, but not interchangeable. In order to create a strong family tree that provides deep roots, comforting shade, sturdy branches to climb, and beautiful leaves, we need to accept God's truth that husbands' and wives' roles are different and sacred.

The Husband's Role Versus the Wife's Role

According to Scripture, husbands are called to do four things: lead, love, care for, and respect their wives.

Look up the following verses. Describe how each one played out in your family of origin. Then write how you want your husband to live out this verse in your marriage.

Ephesians 5:23

    Family of origin:

    Your marriage:

Ephesians 5:25

    Family of origin:

    Your marriage:

Ephesians 5:28

    Family of origin:

    Your marriage:

1 Peter 3:7
Family of origin:

Your marriage:

Husbands have daunting roles, but God also calls wives to fulfill significant important functions within marriage.

Just as you did above, look up the following verses and describe how each one played out in your family of origin. Then write how you want to live out each verse in your own marriage.

Titus 2:4
Family of origin:

Your marriage:

Ephesians 5:33

Family of origin:

Your marriage:

1 Peter 3:1

Family of origin:

Your marriage:

God's Call for Esther in Marriage

In the past I've often felt defeated in my role as a wife. Bible studies, teachers, and well-meaning friends often point to Proverbs 31 as the ideal wife and mother that women should emulate. But let's face it, this woman is often misinterpreted as a picture of impeccability: the Pinterest-perfect, party-planning, business-growing, domestic goddess, the hostess with the mostest, whose fingernails are elegantly polished and clothes are perfectly pressed, and whose children wear color-coordinated, monogrammed clothes to playdates.

Instead of the Proverbs 31 woman, let's look at another woman who provides a great example for married women throughout the ages—Queen Esther. I can hear you now: *What! A beauty-pageant-winning queen as a good example for me? I can barely find time to shave my legs!* Trust me on this one, friends. God gives us all a call in marriage, and Esther is a great example of a woman living out her call.

You may have heard the story of beautiful Queen Esther, the orphan girl raised by her cousin Mordecai and chosen by the salacious King Xerxes for his own pleasure. This young bride's marital obligations consisted of the following duties:

- To conform her physical beauty to the king's liking
- To appear in the presence of the king only when summoned
- To hold only opinions that match those of the king
- To be seen and not heard when in the presence of the king
- To respond to the king only when directly addressed by him
- To respond to the king with the utmost respect, grace, and humility (lest her fate equal that of the late Queen Vashti)

I cannot imagine my entire existence—my physical appearance, thoughts, emotions, likes, and dislikes—all revolving around my husband. I came out of my mother's womb voicing my opinions. I think God knew I wouldn't last ten seconds in Esther's day.

So all goes well in the land of trophy wives and concubines until Cousin Mordy discovers an evil plot by the king's right-hand man, Haman, to wipe out the Jews (Esther 3:8–11; 4:1–2).

When Mordecai implores his cousin to take action, she reminds him of her culture and customs and of her delicate place in the house of glass. Mordecai "sent back this answer: 'Do not think that because you are in the king's house you alone of all the Jews will escape. For if you remain silent at this time, relief and deliverance for the Jews will arise from another place, but you and your father's family will perish. And who knows but that you have come to your royal position for such a time as this?'" (Esther 4:13–14).

Ouch! Thanks for the reality check, Cousin Mordy. As difficult as this message is, sweet Esther needs to hear it. She needs a reminder that her marriage is not for her own comfort. Her role as King Xerxes's wife is a specific, God-ordained position in history.

God gives each of us a specific role in our marriage, family, and community. For the past eleven years I have been a stay-at-home mom and, more recently, a work-at-home mom. I don't pretend to love standing knee-deep in diapers. In fact, many days I have cried, begging God to give me a full-time job and release me from the call of staying home. But then He reminds me of all the ways He has blessed my family because of my time at home with my children. I also reflect on the transformative work He has done in my own life, and I find peace.

Just as Esther was in the right place at the right time to live out God's call for her life, I know I am in the right place at the right time to live out God's call for me. Esther reached a crossroads and had to decide whether she would accept the call. For me, I had to decide many things: Would Brandon and I accept the call to pursue foster care? Would I pursue a writing and speaking ministry instead of taking a job that is more financially secure? For you, the crossroads will look different and the call will be something entirely unique.

Describe the right time and right place in which God has currently placed you.

What is God's call for you in this season of your life?

God's Call for You in Marriage

While it might sound lofty, our marital roles are an opportunity to live out God's call. By fulfilling our roles in marriage, we serve as light in a dark world. No matter what difficulties and decisions we face in our marriages (job, relocation, cancer, miscarriage), we can follow Esther's example and discover God's calling in the midst of our messiness by practicing four things: prayer, patience, obedience, and courage.

First, Esther prays. We see her fasting, but she does so in an effort to keep herself centered in prayer. She also encourages others to pray and fast on her behalf (Esther 4:15–17). Big decisions require big prayers. Esther knows that bucking the cultural system and overturning the king's heart will not happen without divine intervention. So she approaches her heavenly King before approaching her earthly king.

Second, Esther practices patience. She shows self-restraint—in contrast to the king who satisfies his insatiable, ravenous appetite—and waits for an opportune moment at the party. Then she makes her move and approaches him.

Sometimes, we (women or men) want what we want when we want it, and we want it *now!* We often rush in or out of a job, a church, or even a relationship. Instead of praying it out and remaining patient, we opt for a quick fix and exchange one set of problems for another. We need to learn to do less wanting and more waiting.

Next, Esther lives obediently. When Mordecai first tells her she must approach the king, she hesitates. She doesn't want to risk her position—or her life—so she offers a lame excuse about custom and protocol and yada, yada, yada. No doubt Esther feared for her life. But, as we see throughout the Bible, and as we have probably experienced in our own lives, obedience is seldom comfortable, safe, or easy. It almost always requires sacrifice and faith.

How is God calling you to live obediently in your marriage?

What is preventing you from obeying His call?

Finally, Esther is courageous. She reveals Haman's evil plot to destroy the Jews. In doing so she risks her title and her life—yet she saves her people. Every day we wake up and are faced with challenges and fears. We can choose a safe, mundane existence—just going through the motions—or we can choose a life of courage and obedience. Only one of these choices has the power to change the world.

Esther chose a life of courage and saved an entire nation in the process. In what area of your life is God calling you to make a courageous decision?

Submission in Marriage

We have discussed both your husband's role and your role in marriage. Now it's time to tackle the dirty little s-word. My kids think the s-word is *stupid* or *shut up* (they're very sheltered, I know). The s-word I know is much worse. The s-word in every woman's vocabulary is (drumroll, please) . . . *submission*.

Submission has been a hot-button topic for decades. Unfortunately, the world has twisted and abused the word, inciting fear among men and women everywhere. God commanded submission to bring beauty and order into marriage, but spouses use the concept to create a wedge between them or as a weapon against each other. It's time for husbands and wives to reclaim this word that was meant for our benefit, not our demise.

Since you haven't slammed this book shut yet, let's talk about the biblical definition of *submission*. The apostle Paul instructed the people of Ephesus as follows: "The Spirit makes it possible to submit humbly to one another out of respect for the Anointed. Wives, it should be no different with your husbands. Submit to them as you do to the Lord, for God has given husbands a sacred duty to lead as the Anointed leads the church and serves as the head. (The church is His body; He is her Savior.) So wives should submit to their husbands, respectfully, in all things, just as the church yields to the Anointed One" (Eph. 5:21–24 voice).

In verse 21, Paul commands people to "submit humbly to one another." He is speaking generally about submission—in society, in work, and in government—as a foundation for order and peace. The submission he alludes to is the same submission the military uses when talking about rank. Military rank does not determine one's intrinsic value; it does, however, offer stability, function, and order within the organization. Paul asserts that the same is true for our society.

Next, Paul contends that if, in society, we accept this chain of command in general, then it should be no different for wives, who should submit to their husbands, in specific (v. 22). Further, he says we should submit to our husbands just as we submit to the Lord (v. 24). Paul's charge is logical. We warp it into something emotional because of the negative connotation the world spins on the idea of submission.

So let's take a look at what submission is *not*:

- Laying down our opinions and adopting our spouse's
- A loss of our identity
- Giving up our dreams
- Surrendering to our husband no matter what

- Accepting someone's abusive behavior
- Conceding in a stalemate
- Weakness
- Allowing someone to force us to do something

And let's look at what submission *is*:

- Encouraging our husbands in their identity and dreams
- Exercising strength under control (knowing when to speak and when to remain silent; knowing when to act and when to wait)
- Restraining ourselves so that our husbands can lead
- Practicing the wisdom of what's best for the whole, not just for ourselves
- An active choice

What is your reaction to the above list describing submission?

What is your attitude toward submission (e.g., resistant, affirming, angry, something else)?

Queen Esther clearly chose the role of the submissive wife. She also maintained her identity and her opinions. She did not enable wrong behavior in the kingdom and did use her power and position on behalf of God's people. She exercised strength under control. Finally, she showed wisdom in what was best for her people, not just for herself—and she saved an entire generation of Jews in the process.

I know many women would like to exercise submission as Esther did. Maybe you are one of them. Maybe you wonder how you can practice submission and still actively participate in the marriage when your husband wants to sell the house but you don't want to, or when you want to put the kids in private school but your husband doesn't, or when your husband feels emotionally distant and you don't know how to bridge the gap. The answer to such a question has been the topic of many books and is far too complex to answer here. However, we can start by taking these three baby steps:

1. *Embrace joy.* It's easy to develop a resentful spirit in marriage. Give your husband space to lead your family. As much as is possible and reasonable, do it with a joyful heart instead of a resentful spirit. Submission is a choice; we are not powerless.

2. *Use your voice.* Many women think submission equals silence, but that is the Enemy's lie. Submission is compassionately approaching our husbands with kindness and respect that does not undermine them. Submission means honestly explaining our feelings and opinions, then listening and trying to understand. Submission is using our voice to pray for resolution instead of devising plans to get our way.

3. *Remember your significance.* You matter. You are special simply because God created you. Submission does not determine your worth. In fact, submitting to your husband shows how special you truly are. God created you because your husband needed a helper (Gen. 2:18). Your husband needs you! You are vital to his success and his own feelings of self-worth. Never forget that, my friend.

Over the years Brandon and I have muddled our way through submission. It doesn't come easily for me, and it has taken much prayer, Bible study, and conversation to understand how submission works best in our marriage. If submission doesn't come easily to you either, I urge you to not give up. Press on. Grapple with the tough issues. Pray through disagreements. Find a way to come together and strengthen your roots so your trunk becomes solid and your future branches may spread out far and wide.

And before we end our discussion on submission, please hear me, friends: there is a difference between obedience and submission. If you are currently in an abusive relationship, your husband is asking for your obedience, not your submission. Obedience that violates God's Word is never right. Hiding your husband's sinful behavior is not your responsibility. Seek godly counsel from qualified counselors and experts. God wants you to be safe and healthy.

Strengthening Your Roots

1. Review the Bible verses outlining a wife's role in marriage (in the beginning of this chapter). Now list some expectations you have for yourself as a wife. Your expectations can be both abstract (e.g., I plan to be supportive and encouraging) and concrete (e.g., I will cook dinner three times a week).

Examine the list you just made. What are some of your unrealistic expectations? How can you tweak them to make them more likely to occur in your marriage?

How do your expectations align with your gifts, talents, and interests?

Now, on a separate sheet of paper, ask your husband to list his expectations for you as his wife. Compare your lists. Do your expectations match his? If not, how can you come to an agreement?

If you want to go a step further and your husband seems willing, you can also both list your expectations for him as a husband and then compare lists. Remember, I would have saved myself a lot of four-course dinners if Brandon and I had communicated our expectations from the beginning. This is your chance!

2. Do you feel that the Proverbs 31 woman is an unattainable ideal or an encouraging example? Explain.

3. Esther practiced four disciplines that helped her follow God's call in her marriage. Out of these four (prayer, patience, obedience, and courage), which one is most difficult for you to live out?

4. As does Esther's, our marriages serve as a testimony to the world. What does your marriage say to the world?

A WHISPER IN THE WIND
Perfecting the Art of Communication

As a preteen girl, I didn't know how to communicate my pent-up anger and loneliness. I was too scared to voice my emotions. Even though I grew up in a house of yelling people, I knew that if I yelled back I would face serious consequences. So, to express my anger, I slammed my bedroom door. What began as an occasional practice soon turned into my main form of communication—until my mom took my bedroom door off the hinges. Foiled!

I actually think it was a brilliant parenting strategy, and I don't mind recounting it to my children to deter them from trying the same thing. "When did you get your door back?" they ask me.

"Never," I tell them. "We just moved." Foiled again!

Most children learn healthy communication skills as they grow and mature. They learn these skills the same way they learn how to walk, talk, and dress themselves—by watching someone else and then imitating them. This *someone* is generally their parents, who, hopefully, teach their children that healthy communication includes the following:

- Availability
- Listening
- Love
- Patience
- Empathy
- Understanding
- Believing the best in the other person
- Collaborative problem solving
- Giving the benefit of the doubt
- Grace balanced with truth
- A judgment-free zone

Unhealthy Communication

Unfortunately, if you grew up with broken branches, you might never have experienced this type of healthy communication. You might not know how to talk and connect with your spouse in a calm, rational, respectful way that expresses your thoughts and feelings so that you both feel heard and understood.

My family of origin relied on yelling as its main form of communication, but there are many other forms of unhealthy communication in dysfunctional families as well. Take a look at this list and see if anything resonates with you about your family of origin:

- Abusing one spouse or each other (whether emotionally, verbally, or physically)
- Avoiding issues; withdrawing emotionally or physically; refusing to engage
- Blaming
- Criticizing
- Devaluing the other person
- Escalating
- Interrupting; preparing one's argument while the other person is talking
- Intimidating
- Keeping score
- Lying
- Making assumptions
- Manipulating
- Needing total control
- Overpromising and underdelivering
- Raging and throwing things
- Shaming
- Threatening
- Using passive-aggressive comments
- Yelling

Marissa ✺ I come from a family that yells and screams but gets it all out on the table—that battles it out, every man for himself. My husband's family never yells; they avoid their problems.

So there we were in the early years, bringing two completely different styles of communication and conflict resolution to the table, neither healthy. By me, there was a lot of yelling and slamming doors, and by him, there was a lot of not speaking to me then blowing up weeks later for something I didn't even realize bothered him. We had to find a way to meet somewhere in the middle. We had to understand that, for him, yelling was scary and always bad, and, for me, it was always bad and scary when people weren't even talking.

The first month of marriage was pretty tough, to say the least. It took several arguments before we could reflect on our interactions and see where we were going wrong and what changes needed to be made. I am quick to get angry, to run, and to sever relationships when things get tough. I don't have that option anymore, and I am so thankful for that. I had to learn how to cope with that reality though. When everything inside me was screaming, "Run, run, run! Get away, because I can handle it on my own," I had to learn to listen from the depths of my soul and stay and remember that the brokenness there is healing. And somehow I had to learn how to communicate all those feelings to my husband to help him understand where I was at in those moments. That took some time and pain, but it was so worth it.

When I married Brandon, I stopped slamming the door, but I replaced this dysfunctional way of communicating with other destructive habits, such as hanging up the phone while he was talking or refusing to engage in conversation altogether. I did these things because, even though I had matured (clearly in years, not in emotion), the root issue remained: I still got angry, but I felt too scared to express my emotions.

Changing lifelong patterns of destructive communication is difficult but not impossible. Embracing empathy when you've only experienced criticism is a daunting task but not an insurmountable one. Engaging in healthy confrontation when you've spent your life running in fear is not only possible, it is God's desire for you. All of this requires two skills: listening and encouraging. Both skills are rooted in applying and understanding Scripture.

Look at the lists of healthy and unhealthy communication skills (pp. 111–112).

1. Place the letter O next to the communication skills that describe your family of origin.

2. Place the letter M next to the communication skills that describe your marriage.

How have your family of origin's unhealthy communication skills affected your communication with your own family?

In contrast, how have your family of origin's healthy communication skills affected your communication practices in your marriage?

Healthy Communication

I love this verse in the book of James: "Listen, open your ears, harness your desire to speak, and don't get worked up into a rage so easily, my brothers and sisters" (1:19 VOICE). When I read the word *harness*, I envision a jockey controlling his horse, much as we must control our speech. Just as the jockey must harness the horse to keep her calm, focused, driven, and in her lane so she doesn't run into another horse, we must tame our own words and behavior so we don't run over people. We want our words to be calm and focused, lest we hurt ourselves or someone else as a result of our gossip, anger, or half-truths.

James also mentions the word *rage*. For many of us, rage was a normal part of life in our family of origin. We awoke to the noise of our parents breaking dishes and yelling in the kitchen. We watched our dad physically hurt our mom—or maybe vice versa. We endured the hateful or spiteful words our parents spewed at us over the years. Rage was not something we saw in an R-rated movie; rage was our everyday experience.

We need to master the art of listening to our spouse—even a loud spouse. When we interrupt someone, we invalidate them and indirectly communicate these things:

- What you want to say is insignificant, trivial, or even worthless.
- What I want to say is more important than what you want to say.
- My point of view is more important than your point of view.
- I am more important than you.
- My needs are more important than your needs.
- I am the dominant person in this relationship.

If we want to understand our spouses, we must listen. We must cast aside our own agendas and put their needs first. This others-first mentality serves the best interests of the marriage, because when our husbands' needs are met, they will feel fulfilled and naturally desire to meet our needs. As they love us well, we will feel cared for and more inclined to listen to our husband's needs . . . and the cycle continues.

Marissa ✽ We know how to talk to each other now, and, more importantly, we know how to listen.

In what situations do you interrupt your husband?

How can you do a better job of listening to your husband?

A Good Word

Listening is vital, but so is spurring one another on with encouraging words. The apostle Paul warned the Ephesians to keep their conversation under control. "Don't let even one rotten word seep out of your mouths. Instead, offer only fresh words that build others up when they need it most. That way your good words will communicate grace to those who hear them" (Eph. 4:29 VOICE).

I like the translation of this Bible verse in *The Voice* because the word *seep* paints a perfect picture of what happens in our lives. Most of us wouldn't admit to being gossips, but most of us do share "prayer requests" because that's what good Christian women do. Be careful about what you share with your friends, especially when it pertains to your marriage. Respect your husband, his honor, and the privacy of your marriage.

Friends, husband-bashing seems to be a favorite pastime for some women, and I urge you to not make your husband's shortcomings the topic of your next book club or bunco group. Honor your husband with your speech as you hope he is honoring you.

There is a story that clearly illustrates the consequences of our careless, and even disparaging, words. "It is said that a man once came to Mohammed and asked how he could make amends for falsely accusing a friend. Mohammed told him to put a feather on every doorstep in the village. Next day he told the man to collect them. 'But that is impossible,' said the man, 'the wind has scattered them beyond recall!' [Mohammed] replied, 'So is it with your reckless words.'"[1]

Maybe reckless words aren't your downfall, but you find encouragement generally difficult. Perhaps you're not the touchy-feely type and you feel awkward expressing that kind of emotion. Or maybe expressing yourself as a child, whether positively or negatively, resulted in eating alone in the dining room, being banished to your room, or physical punishment too painful to articulate. You have learned to guard your words as a means of emotional survival.

Paul's words are for you too. He writes, "Use your heads as you live and work among outsiders. Don't miss a trick. Make the most of every opportunity. Be gracious in your speech. The goal is to bring out the best in others in a conversation, not put them down, not cut them out" (Col. 4:5 MSG).

When Paul writes "use your heads," he is saying that communication is a skill. We cannot rely on our emotions, which are fickle, wearying, and untrustworthy. We must use our heads and work with the wisdom and truth God has given us. We might not have seen healthy communication when we were growing up, but we can rely on God's Word to teach us healthy communication skills. After all, we might be someone's only window to the kingdom of God.

How can you encourage your husband this week? You might think of one significant way or five small ways. Make a plan to accomplish this within the week.

A Healthy Heart

Jesus tells the disciples that emotions play a huge role in communication. "But the things that come out of a person's mouth come from the heart, and these defile them. For out of the heart come evil thoughts—murder, adultery, sexual immorality, theft, false testimony, slander" (Matt. 15:18–19). What you feel affects what you say.

In part 1 we talked about memory triggers. These triggers not only bring memories to the surface but also certain emotions; these emotions affect your attitude, which determines your actions. When your communication derails, ask yourself, *Am I feeling . . .*

- afraid?
- angry?
- frustrated?
- insecure?
- lonely?
- neglected?
- sad?
- taken advantage of?
- worried?
- _____?

Simply saying to a flower, "Bloom!" or to a tree, "Grow!" will produce zero results. Understanding its needs, however, and then providing appropriate soil, sun, and rain will result in healthy change and growth.

The same is true for you. You cannot will yourself to change your old communication patterns. You must understand the emotions behind the words. Once you identify your emotions, you will understand the motives sparking your actions and words.

You might also consider talking to someone about your communication patterns, whether your spouse, a friend, or a mentor. Devise a plan to help you defuse your emotions before they overwhelm you. Here are some ideas:

- Call someone who can help you sort through a tough situation.
- Go for a drive.
- Go for a run or walk.
- Write in a journal.
- Listen to praise and worship music.
- Pray and ask God to change your perspective and emotions.
- Take a yoga or exercise class you enjoy.
- _____.

In what ways do you find your emotions affecting the way you communicate with your spouse?

A Gentle Tone

In today's culture filled with texting, emailing, and social media, we can be cowards. We can break up with a boyfriend, resign from a job, fire a nanny, or criticize a friend without ever making eye contact.

That's why I love the verse that reads, "There is so much I would like to say to you, but I do not want to say it with ink and pen. I expect us to be together soon and talk about these things face-to-face" (3 John 13–14 VOICE). Let's ditch the texting and emailing and instead engage in real-life conversations with people about important matters. Let's meet people for coffee or invite them over for dinner. If we have something significant to say but can't make the time or effort to say it in person, then we probably should not communicate the words via technology.

If we need to communicate something important to our spouses, we should avoid texting or emailing. This is a great rule, but you may find it tough to carry out. Perhaps you dated for a month and communicated via text before officially holding hands, but trust me, marriage is the big league. It's time to ramp up your communication skills and *talk* it out. Whether at dinner or while cozying up on a couch, express what's on your heart and mind, but say it face to face.

If practice makes perfect, then you will improve in the art of confrontation over time. You will become more aware of your tone of voice and nonverbal cues—how you stand, gesture, position your arms and legs, move your eyes and facial muscles, and much more. You may have a quiet voice but loud body language if you cross your arms or make large gestures with your hands and arms. Pointing your finger at the other person and putting your hands on your hips are also considered loud body language. These nonverbal cues communicate that you feel defensive, argumentative, and combative. If you don't learn to control what you communicate, you may find that your husband will tune you out before you reach your most important point . . . an emotionally self-protective move on his part.

Think about your communication, then answer the next set of questions.

When it comes to communication, are you loud and chaotic (getting louder and more agitated as the conversation progresses), quiet and withdrawn (almost never voicing your opinion), or calm and diplomatic (thoughtfully trying to reach a sensible resolution)? Give a specific example that explains how you most often communicate.

Consider the options listed above. How does your husband communicate? Describe a specific example.

How do your styles of communication work together?

How could you both improve your communication through changing your tone?

Communication Tools

I'm not exactly sure why our family needs four toolboxes in the garage, but my husband assures me we do. When it comes to communication, we need a toolbox too (but probably one, not four). Here are a few tools to help fill your communication toolbox.

Talk Time

Take time once a day to talk. There's nothing earth-shattering about this concept except that couples don't do it. Mornings are rushed, getting everyone to school and work. Evenings are busy with dinner, sports, activities, and homework. We don't expect a plant to grow without watering it, yet we often wonder why our marriages don't flourish when we don't pour regular times of intentional communication into them.

Talk time can be scheduled or spontaneous. Scheduling talk time can bring comfort because you know you can count on it, but some people like to take advantage of small moments, such as when you're both brushing your teeth or folding laundry. The goal is to find even ten minutes a day to talk about more than the kids and your jobs. You'll be surprised how connected you'll feel after investing even a few minutes a day to focus on each other.

Consider the following sample questions to get you started talking:

- What is God teaching you?
- What is the best thing that happened to you today?
- What was the most challenging thing that happened to you today?
- What are we doing really well right now?
- What can we do better right now?
- How can I serve you better?
- What do you hope to accomplish this week? This month? This year?

State of the Union

The "state of the union," unlike talk time, does need to be scheduled (sorry all you free spirits). This meeting occurs about once or twice a month (although I know some people who meet weekly).

During this meeting you can discuss schedules, finances, child-rearing, and major decisions affecting your marriage and family such as job changes, selling the house, or vacations. But don't think you need to confine the conversation to logistics. Feel free to talk openly about your fears, worries, concerns, excitements, and more. Over time these meetings will help you gain greater emotional intimacy and trust.

Rating Scale

Our dear friend Cindy, who's a professional counselor and author, taught us a rating scale for our conversations, and it revolutionized our marriage. This tool is helpful because sometimes we feel the need to escalate a conversation's intensity by using a loud voice or repeating our viewpoint just to feel heard (although the other person is probably tuning us out). By using the rating scale (*one* means the subject is not very important, *five* means it's extremely important), we communicate the intensity of the subject before the conversation begins.

For instance, I wanted to talk to Brandon about the possibility of sending one of our kids to a private school. This was a very important issue, and I needed to prepare Brandon. So I texted him: "We need to talk tonight. Level 5 convo. Don't worry, you're not in trouble. Ha ha."

Conversations such as, "Where are we going on vacation this year?" or "Should we buy a new couch?" might rank on level one or two. The key to making the rating scale work is to evaluate the true importance of every situation.

Brandon and I mentored a young married couple, Jeremy and Suzanne (not their real names), a few years ago, and we asked them to use the rating scale to eliminate some negative behaviors such as yelling and throwing household objects. The next week they came back, and we were eager to find out if the rating scale worked.

"It was awful," Jeremy said.

"What happened?" we asked, disappointed.

"She rated everything a five!" he hollered.

"That's because everything *is* a level five!" Suzanne yelled back.

They realized the one flaw with the rating scale—overinflation. You cannot rate every issue a level five. Be honest with yourself and with your spouse.

Strengthening Your Roots

1. In this chapter I talk about how our unhealthy communication might sometimes be a condition of the heart. In what ways does your unhealthy or negative communication reflect the condition of your heart?

2. I offer different ways to keep your emotions in check so you don't respond negatively to others (praying, taking a walk, etc.). Out of the list, which tactic most appealed to you? Explain.

3. How does your tone (verbal or nonverbal) affect your relationships? What steps might you take to improve this area?

4. Review the communication tools listed in this chapter. Are you currently implementing any tools? If so, which one(s)? If not, which tool(s) would you like to incorporate into your marriage?

How is this affecting your relationship?

THE CALM AFTER THE STORM
Learning Conflict Management

When Brandon and I dated in college, our only argument occurred when he tutored me in finance. At the end of the semester, I earned my first and only college D. It's a good thing D stands for D-O-N-E because I think Brandon was more interested in spending time with me than making sure I understood finance. I'm just saying. Other than our finance-induced spat, we were a pretty easy-going couple.

After we married, however, we made up for lost time. Our first few months of marriage were steeped in arguments because neither of us knew how to handle conflict. I had experienced years of volatile, abusive battles in my family of origin so when a conflict arose, I thought fighting was the only way to solve our problems. Yet the minute Brandon began to talk the problem through, I became scared and retreated—I tucked my head into my turtle shell, which is far from my usually honest, direct, authoritative personality.

Brandon, on the other hand, had never seen conflict when he was growing up—not an argument, a heated discussion, or a disagreement. So the first time I exploded and then withdrew, he thought we were doomed for divorce. He tried to draw me out of my protective shell to initiate conversation, but I responded with a fiery comeback, after which he felt defeated, I retreated again, and the cycle repeated itself.

There were no magical fixes, but over time we learned to make several changes that greatly impacted our marriage:

- Brandon consistently repeated the phrase, "We're on the same team," which helped me realize that Brandon was not my enemy.
- We attended a young married class every Sunday morning at church, which gave us practical tools that we applied at home.
- We read marriage books—together and independently—which gave us more tools to implement.
- We prayed together and separately for each other. No marriage will thrive without the power of the Holy Spirit's intervention.

Conflict in marriage is inevitable, but it can be healthy and fruitful when handled correctly. Let's take a look at how God wants us to manage our conflict.

Do you fear conflict and avoid it, or face it head on?

Overcoming Fight, Flight, or Freeze

For many of us, *conflict* was—and maybe still is—a scary word. If you grew up in a home characterized by verbal assaults, physical abuse, controlling behaviors, criticism, or continual tension, you understand. Everyone responds to conflict in one of three ways: fight, flight, or freeze.

Many strong-willed kids respond to conflict with the fight response. If you stood up for yourself by engaging in verbal defense, only to realize your parents held all the power, you fought. If you tried to protect your mom from your abusive dad, you fought.

If you ran away and hid in your closet when your parents' fighting erupted or stayed away from the house as much as possible trying to avoid the next world war, you reacted with a flight response. If you stood motionless, paralyzed with fear as your parents' arguments escalated, you froze.

However you handled the situation, you assumed a burden that should never have been yours to carry. Your response to conflict today most likely mimics your childhood response of fight, flight, or freeze. Fortunately, we can change these patterns if we understand the concept of conflict management.

Good friend and communications professor, Dr. Blair Browning, introduced Brandon and me to the concept of conflict management. This philosophy is simple: In life and in marriage, conflict is inevitable. We might not always be able to resolve our conflict, but we can learn to manage it. Whoa! That's some truth telling right there!

In our previous chapter we discussed communication, which is a two-way exchange of information, ideas, and feelings as a way to reach a mutual understanding. It's a way to connect people and bring them closer to one another, not divide them. In marriage, we communicate in order to understand our spouses on a deeper level and grow closer to them.

Conflict management is a way to recognize and deal with disagreements in a rational, balanced, and effective way. People use healthy, effective communication skills to achieve conflict management. If we want to handle conflict well, we must first communicate well. Both are learned skills that improve with time and practice.

From Conflict to Intimacy

The beauty of covenant marriage is that everything we do and say should point us toward deeper intimacy, whether that's date nights, vacation getaways, talk times, or state of the union talks. Even conflict, once resolved, draws us toward our spouses.

Karen ✸ It's difficult, even if you're both committed and working at it. Conflict is the price we pay for deeper intimacy.

If we want a mediocre marriage with surface level conversation, then we will avoid conflict at all costs. But if we want greater intimacy with our spouses, we will face conflict head on.

Natalie ✸ You won't always agree with your spouse. Even if you communicate and conflict well, there will still be things you don't see the same way, and that's actually a good thing. I don't want a "one brain" marriage. Yes, I want to be unified with my husband, but diversity is actually beneficial, not divisive, in our marriage. One of us isn't right and the other wrong. It's simply a difference of perspective. It's taken me way too long to figure that out.

When I wrote *If You Could See as Jesus Sees*, I had many doubts swirling around my feeble brain, such as, *I am just a nobody writer. No one will read this. No one will buy it.* I believed the request I received to write it was a fluke and I was a joke. I listened to the lies of the Enemy and certainly didn't see myself as Jesus saw me. But Brandon did. He saw me. He encouraged me. He reassured me. He believed I could accomplish more than I believed I could. And quite honestly, I didn't receive his cheering well. It caused conflict and frustration, but in the end it brought us into greater emotional intimacy.

I think most of us want husbands who differ from us and make up for our deficiencies. We want husbands who are strong where we are weak and weak where we are strong. God knows His people are diverse, but He still longs for us to be unified.

Fall is my favorite season for many reasons; cooler weather means super cute clothes (good riddance, swimsuit season), college football, roaring fires in the fireplace, and changing leaves. Some people like the fullness of green in the spring, but I adore the many hues of autumn, orange, yellow, brown, and red. The pounds of leaves filling our yard are unique and beautiful and remind me that with each new season, God makes all things new. Just as each leaf is different, so are God's people. Just as these leaves live in unity on tree branches, we must live in unity with our spouses. Yes, we might have seasons when we fall down, but God will pick us back up and restore us. "How good and pleasant it is when God's people live together in unity!" (Ps. 133:1).

In what ways have you experienced conflict leading to intimacy in your marriage?

Fighting Well

If you have children, then you know conflict is inevitable. We have a saying in our house, Our children play well and fight well. They build a fort one minute in perfect harmony, then break into war the next because someone stole a favorite toy. With five children, we expect conflict, but we want to teach our kids how to battle well. The same skills are needed in marriage.

Below are suggested guidelines to help you fight well when engaging your spouse in conflict.

1. *Tell the truth.* "I would never lie," you might say. But what if your spouse asks, "How are you doing?" If you say "Fine," even when you're so angry you could spit fiery arrows, you're lying to your spouse. Whenever you feel angry, sad, depressed, worried, or scared, but you say you feel fine, you are lying and robbing your spouse of emotional intimacy. "The Lord detests lying lips, but he delights in people who are trustworthy" (Prov. 12:22).
2. *Face it—don't ignore it.* Don't tuck your head into your shell as I did. Accept the fact that conflict will arise, and when it does, face the problem. Sometimes it even helps to play out the worst-case scenario in your mind. Reality is almost never as horrible as what we imagine.

3. *Develop a team approach.* As I said in the previous chapter, Brandon's mantra during our first year of marriage was, We're on the same team. In a covenant marriage, even when you argue there should be no winner and no loser, because you're on the same team. In every disagreement you should work toward determining what's best for your marriage and what steps are needed to accomplish that with unity.

4. *Accept your differences.* The two of you approach situations, ideas, and problems differently because you have different personalities, perspectives, backgrounds, and ways of communicating.

   If a small issue arises, accept your differences and move on. If a more pressing issue comes up, that issue might be too huge to solve in two hours. Don't rush through conflict just because the clock is ticking.

Catherine ❁ I wish I had known that we would always fight over the same issues. My husband struggled to do dishes when we first got married, and he still does. It's the little, nitpicky, day-to-day things that can drive a person crazy if you let them.

5. *Decide on the right time for conflict.* Engage in conflict when distractions are low and energy is high. Eleven o'clock at night or ten minutes before little Timmy's soccer game is not the right time to bring up an issue. Schedule talk time or a state of the union and address the subject at that time.

6. *Identify the core issue.* Don't get bogged down in the details of the situation. Ask yourself, "What is the core issue?" Maybe it's not really about your husband working late or forgetting date night or not responding to texts. Maybe the core issue is that you feel insecure and neglected. Maybe it's even deeper than that. Maybe your dad had an affair, and you're starting to think your husband's behavior indicates adultery. Talk about the core issue.

7. *Stick to the core issue.* Don't get historical by bringing up things that happened last month or last year. And don't keep score with

a running total of all the ways your spouse has hurt you. Forgive and move on. "[Love] is not self-seeking, it is not easily angered, it keeps no record of wrongs" (1 Cor. 13:5).

8. *Avoid attacking your spouse's character.* Remember, you're on the same team and you have identified the core issue. If you keep these two things in mind, you will be less likely to insult or injure your spouse.

9. *Use* I *statements, not* you *statements.* I am feeling hurt and neglected, or I need more time with you, will go a lot further than You always work late, or You're never at home. Learn to express yourself without putting your spouse on the defensive. "A gentle answer turns away wrath, but a harsh word stirs up anger" (Prov. 15:1).

10. *Identify your end goal.* Once you know the core issue, identify what you hope to achieve at the end of the argument. Maybe you want to schedule one date night per week or establish a budget. Be specific about your end goal so that you both understand each other's expectations.

11. *Brainstorm solutions, then solve the problem.* Brandon always says, "There are no bad ideas in brainstorming." I beg to differ. Some ideas are really bad (I won't say whether they're his ideas or mine—ha ha!). The point is, when you disagree and are searching for a solution, propose all possible resolutions, and discuss how they would affect you, your spouse, and your marriage. After you've had time to process, decide which solution will work and implement it. If none of the solutions seem appropriate, continue brainstorming or seek a third party's opinion.

12. *Seek wise counsel if necessary.* Seeking wise counsel is not the same as exposing your conflict publicly. Seek counsel when you hit a brick wall. When you have discussed the conflict and still disagree, you need an unbiased third party's opinion. This should be someone you both trust: a friend, mentor, pastor, or professional counselor. I advise against choosing a parent because they are generally biased. While they may be loving and well-meaning, they carry too much history and will typically side with their child.

Mama Bear and Dear Old Dad are also slower to forgive our spouses than we are.

13. *Don't expose your conflict publicly.* More aptly put, don't air out your dirty laundry on social media or over a glass of wine with a group of girlfriends. Brandon and I have encountered many couples who post their marital debates on Facebook for the court of public opinion. There is no better way to destroy intimacy in your marriage than to bring other people into your private conversations. Keep your personal conflict private.

14. *Forgive one another.* Forgiveness is the crux of the gospel, yet we often fail to make it the foundation of our marriage. We will never gain emotional intimacy with our spouses if we cannot forgive their shortcomings or their failures. "And forgive us our sins, as we have forgiven those who sin against us" (Matt. 6:12 NLT).

Of the fourteen guidelines above, circle the ones you are currently practicing in your marriage.

Of those you are not currently practicing, which one will be most difficult for you to implement? Why?

Which one(s) do you think will be fairly simple to implement? Why?

Conflict Management Tools

Just as we need tools for healthy communication, we need tools for conflict management. Here are a few for you and your spouse to try:

Time-Out Technique

In the book of Ephesians Paul writes, "Be angry and do not sin; do not let the sun go down on your anger" (4:26 ESV). However, some couples take this to the extreme and stay up until the wee hours when eventually one person concedes out of sheer exhaustion.

Brandon and I agree that God doesn't want us to go to bed harboring anger, bitterness, and resentment toward our spouse. But we also believe not every argument can be solved in one night. Sometimes you need to hit the pause button and revisit an issue the next day. Before your next conflict (and who knows when that might be), consider the following guidelines for a time-out:

- Come to an emotional plateau where you can honestly say to each other, "OK, we disagree on this, but I know we still love each other and want the best for our marriage. Let's sleep on it and revisit this in the morning when we're both thinking more clearly."
- Agree on the specific day and time to revisit the issue.
- Follow through. You *must* reunite at the appointed day and time and reassess the issue.
- Resolve the issue with a solution and forgiveness.

In what ways would taking a time-out from your argument benefit your marriage?

Catherine ❋ I grew up in an abusive home—verbally, emotionally, and physically abusive. Things weren't dealt with peacefully or well. There was a lot of yelling and accusing and spanking, and there was a lot of walking on eggshells and wondering what would set my mom off. And honestly, I am still learning to respond to my husband and children differently.

Speaker–Listener Technique

With this tool, one person assumes the role of speaker, and the other person assumes the role of listener.[1] The speaker takes the floor. She talks in small chunks, no more than one to two sentences at a time. She expresses only her feelings, thoughts, or concerns (never her perceptions or interpretations) using *I* statements. For example:

> SPEAKER: "I feel hurt when you side with your mother instead of defending me."

Notice the speaker does not make *you* statements such as, "You always defend your mother. You never defend me." She also does not offer perceptions such as, "When you spend so much time with your mother, I know you love her more than you love me." The speaker sticks to her feelings and concerns.

The listener may not, at any time, interrupt or rebut the speaker. He also may not get defensive. The listener will have a chance to express his disagreements when he has the floor. The listener's job is to listen and understand. When the speaker is done speaking, the listener paraphrases what the speaker just said.

> LISTENER: "So what I hear you saying is that when I side with my mother instead of defending you, it really hurts your feelings. Is that correct?"

Once the listener is finished speaking, the speaker determines if the listener's interpretation was correct. If so, the speaker may speak again. This pattern may continue one or two more times.

SPEAKER: "Yes. That's correct. I also feel hurt when I make plans for us and your mom intrudes on our plans and you don't intervene. I would like for you to defend me by letting her know that we already have plans."

LISTENER: "So what you're saying is that when my mom intrudes on our plans, it really hurts your feelings."

SPEAKER: "No, what I said is that I feel hurt when I make plans for us and your mom intrudes, and *you don't intervene*. I would like for you to defend me by letting her know that we already have plans."

LISTENER: "Oh, OK. Let me see if I hear you now. You said that what hurts your feelings is not that my mom intrudes on our plans, but that I don't intervene. You would like me to defend you by letting her know we already have plans."

Then the speaker and listener switch roles.

SPEAKER: "Yes! That's it. You can take the floor now."

Both people need to stay on topic and not try to solve the problem right away. The point of this exercise is simply to listen and understand one another.

Both conflict management tools require cooperation and practice, but over time they will teach you healthy ways of conflicting that will eventually bring you into a closer relationship with one another.

Strengthening Your Roots

1. How did your family deal with conflict?

How has that affected the way you deal with conflict now that you are an adult?

2. Do you agree that conflict can bring you and your spouse into greater emotional intimacy? Explain.

3. Refer to the list of conflict management tools. How can you implement the time-out and the speaker-listener techniques in your relationship? Explain.

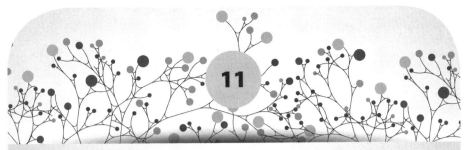

11

YOUR PRIVATE GARDEN

Cultivating Physical Intimacy in Your Marriage

I remember "the talk" almost too vividly. I was in the third grade and completely blindsided. My single mom had to give both my brother and me "the birds and the bees" talk by herself. We didn't have a dad around to teach my brother how to shave, when to use deodorant, or how to approach girls. It was all up to my mom to reveal this world of wonder to both of us. But she was a nurse, so this sort of thing was totally her jam.

Mom sat us both down—together. Ugh. With textbooks. Double ugh. I had no idea what was about to go down, but I knew by her tone it was something serious. She proceeded to tell us all the different names for sex, ranging from G-rated to R-rated terms. I still remember the words ringing in my ears. I knew she was preparing me for the real world, but while she gabbed away like this was all completely normal, I desperately wanted to hide under the couch.

Then she moved on to technical pictures and diagrams that were awkward and off-limits in my nine-year-old, prudish mind. The entire conversation was insanely unbearable with my thirteen-year-old brother sitting next to me. But at least I can say I received a thorough sex education.

I asked Brandon how old he was when his parents gave him the talk.

"I think I'm still waiting," he said. Maybe that's why we have five kids.

Needless to say, a woman's exposure to sex as a child greatly impacts her attitude toward sex as an adult.

What was your mom's attitude toward sex when you were growing up?

What was your dad's attitude toward sex when you were growing up?

Did your mom talk to you about sex when you were younger? If so, was it a one-time conversation or many ongoing conversations? How did those conversations go? Were they comfortable? Awkward for her? Awkward for you? Describe here.

I admit this chapter was not on my radar when I first pitched this book to my publisher. However, the more I talked with women from broken branches, the more I discovered a common thread: a failure to connect physically with a spouse.

Catherine ❋ Weirdly, I think the physical aspect has always been the hardest part of marriage for me. Maybe I watched inappropriate movies as a kid, or maybe I've repressed something. Honestly, I have no idea how this problem is tied to my background, but it's a huge struggle for me.

Something unique in the hardwiring of women from dysfunctional backgrounds prevents us from embracing a rich, fulfilling physical relationship with our husbands. We love them. We desire intimacy with them. Yet, a dense forest of family history, past experiences, and personality differences separates us. After talking with these women, I was determined to figure out why this forest had formed and how to cut down some trees so we could plant a fertile garden of emotional and physical intimacy in our marriages.

Early Exposure to Sex

Before texting, people actually talked on the phone. Crazy. While I played near her, my mom used to talk on the phone to her girlfriends about life, love, and who knows what else. One such time I wandered into the kitchen while she sat at the table chatting away. I plopped down on the floor next to her and tried repeatedly to get her attention. When none of my adorable tricks worked, I blurted out with my cutest, most precocious smile, "Whatcha doing? Talking about sex again?"

Now mind you, I was five at the time and had no idea what sex was, but I knew it was something women talked about with their girlfriends because I'd overheard my mom talking about it on the phone many times (remember, she's a nurse and perfectly comfortable with this subject). Well, apparently whatever sex was, it was not OK for precocious five-year-olds to talk about.

"Where did you hear that word?" my mom asked in shock. Her abrupt reaction scared me. I could tell I'd said something wrong, but I wasn't sure what. I was afraid if I admitted that I'd heard the word from her, then I would get into trouble. I didn't know what to say.

"Where did you hear that word?" she repeated louder this time.

"From *The Facts of Life*," I blurted out. I felt terrible for blaming Blair, Jo, Tootie, and Natalie, but I didn't know what else to do. I watched this eighties sitcom at my babysitter's house every day, and after seeing so many episodes, it was the first thing that popped into my head.

"Well, unless you want me to tell you that you can't watch that show anymore, you won't say that word again," my mom said. "Now go play so I can finish talking." I quickly ran out of the kitchen, taking several important lessons with me:

- Sex is bad.
- I should not talk about sex.
- If I say the word *sex* again, I will get into trouble.
- Sex is something we must cover up and lie about.

In Dr. Kevin Leman's book *Sheet Music*, he states that all couples come into marriage with a "rule book," or an unwritten list of unconscious rules about sex. Many things influence what goes into our rule books, including our parents' views on sex, past sexual abuse, and birth order. Leman writes, "The last determiner of your rulebook . . . consists of your early childhood memories. Those early events (when you were in third grade or younger) helped shape your expectations about life and about the way things should be done. You learned either that the world is a safe place . . . or a dangerous place. You developed the assumption that people will either treat you with kindness . . . or betray you and threaten you."[1]

If we come from a dysfunctional family, our sex education was probably more "community college" and less "ivy league." Maybe some of the scenarios below bring back memories from your own childhood:

- You walked in on your dad taking a shower. Or maybe he walked in on you (accidentally or not).
- Your mom had a revolving door of boyfriends spending the night, or your dad had a long list of girlfriends who would sleep over.
- Your brother and his friends teased you about your maturing body, or maybe they did more than just tease.
- You stumbled upon pornography and gave it more than a passing glance.
- You endured years of sexual abuse by a trusted family friend but were too scared to tell anyone.

Elyse ✳ As a child, I endured repeated sexual encounters but was unable to call it abuse for years. I had some pastoral counseling in college but really didn't understand the comprehensive long-term effects the abuse would have on me. My husband and I committed ourselves to abstinence until marriage, so I did not expect flashbacks to occur once we became intimate. The combination of my childhood sexual abuse and the emotional, mental, and physical abuse I received at the hands of my mom was really brutal. I battled control, manipulation, self-preservation, defensiveness, name-calling, lying, low sex drive, horrible boundaries, and anger.

What was your earliest exposure to sex—either the subject or the physical act?

What early "lessons" did you learn about sex?

Sex and the Media

My friend and fellow broken branch, Catherine, and I talk a lot about the horror movies, gratuitous flicks, and all-around inappropriate shows we watched as kids. We stayed up until two in the morning watching *Nightmare on Elm Street*, *Friday the 13th*, *Fatal Attraction*, and *Revenge of the Nerds*. It's a wonder we made it out of our teens mentally and emotionally intact.

There's much value in monitoring what programs our children watch and what materials they read, as studies show that early exposure to sex can taint our views on sex and intimacy. In fact, one study published in *The Western Journal of Medicine* reported, "Adolescents use the media as sources of information about sex, drugs, AIDS, and violence as well as to learn how to behave in relationships."[2] Other studies contain more interesting facts about teens, media, and sexual behavior:

- "Boys who were exposed to sexually explicit media were three times more likely to engage in oral sex and intercourse two years after exposure than non-exposed boys."[3]
- "Young girls exposed to sexual content in the media were twice as likely to engage in oral sex and one and a half times more likely to have intercourse."[4]
- "Teens who listened to music with degrading sexual references were more likely to have sex than those who had less exposure."[5]
- "More than 66 percent of boys and 40 percent of girls reported wanting to try some of the sexual behaviors they saw in the media (and by high school, many had done so), which increases the risk of sexually transmitted diseases and unwanted pregnancies."[6]
- Pornography is a $97 billion industry globally, with $10 to 12 billion of its profits coming from the United States.[7]
- "For some people, habitual use of pornography may prompt a desire for more violent or deviant material, including depictions of rape, torture or humiliation. If people seek to act out what they see, they may be more likely to commit sexual assault, rape or child molestation."[8]

Sexual sin runs rampant throughout our society and our families, so while these behaviors may not describe you, they might depict someone in your life—a parent, a sibling, a cousin, or a friend.

Mainstream media also flood our culture with sexualized messages through commercials, television shows, movies, books, magazines, and the Internet. It convinces youth that early sexual experimentation is normal and widespread, and it portrays sex as casual, unprotected, and free of consequences. This lifestyle encourages young people to engage in sexual activity long before they are emotionally, socially, or intellectually ready.

Many women from broken branches learned at a young age that sex was not a sacred virtue. Whether they were exposed to pornography, suffered from sexual abuse, witnessed inappropriate sexual behavior in the home, or engaged in sexual activity at a young age, they often struggle to embrace a healthy sexual identity now that they are married. Maybe this sounds all-too familiar to you. God knows the long-term consequences of sexual sin, and He wants to protect His children from this pain, which is why Paul writes, "It is God's will that you should be sanctified: that you should avoid sexual immorality" (1 Thess. 4:3). For some of you, sexual immorality was unavoidable because no one protected your young eyes, minds, and bodies from it when you couldn't protect yourselves.

How has the media's portrayal of sex affected your view of sex?

How has the media's portrayal of sex affected physical intimacy with your husband?

Early Bonding

When people find out I'm a foster mom, they often respond by saying, "Oh, I could never do that." I understand what they mean—they can't stand the thought of loving a child who might leave them. This is the tension foster parents live with every day. I understand the tension, I really do. However, Brandon and I believe someone needs to love these children. Someone needs to welcome them into their home and into their family. Someone needs to rock them at night, teach them how to eat with a fork, help them with their homework, and reassure them that mommies and daddies are not to be feared—even if it causes us a little heartache. God calls the church to love these children because no matter how many tears foster parents shed after a child leaves, our sorrow is nothing compared to the pain that child has endured.

Bringing foster children into our homes is also important because it teaches these children how to bond. You might not have realized it, but we gain the ability to form intimate relationships in early childhood. When a mother holds and rocks her baby, she teaches that baby security. When a dad tucks his son in at bedtime, he teaches him love and protection. When parents encourage their children with positive words, they teach them confidence and self-worth.

If, however, a mother passes out on the couch with a drink in her hand every night, she teaches her son that he must care for himself because no one else will do it. If a dad abandons his wife and children and starts a new family, he teaches his children that they are replaceable and insignificant. When parents spend more time fighting than they do parenting, their children learn that marriage is unsafe and untrustworthy.

If we do not experience bonding, trust, and love early on in life, then we subconsciously resist intimacy—emotional, spiritual, or physical—as we mature. We disconnect from our feelings because someone, early on, taught us that it is safer to care for ourselves than to rely on someone else. Sometimes we assume the worst in people instead of hoping for the best, and often, without even realizing it, we punish our spouses for the crimes of our family tree.

Regarding physical intimacy (which includes more than the act of sex), we fear giving our spouses access to our most sacred possessions: our bodies. If we couldn't trust our parents with our most basic needs when we were children (unconditional love, safety, attention, security, a stable place to live, enough food to eat), we will not trust our spouses with our most basic needs as adults (love, safety, stability, kindness, security, affirmation, connection, trust). We might not make a conscious choice to avoid physical intimacy; rather, we are persuaded by something lying deep within the recesses of our minds. Avoiding physical intimacy and connection with our spouse, however, is not what God wants for our marriages, which is why the apostle Paul addresses this very topic with the people in Corinth. "Each man should feel free to join together in sexual intimacy with his own wife, and each woman should join with her own husband. Husbands and wives have reciprocal duties. Each husband has the responsibility to meet his wife's sexual desires, and each wife should do the same for her husband. In marriage neither the husband nor the wife should act as if his or her body is private property— your bodies now belong to one another, and together they are whole. (1 Cor. 7:2–4 VOICE)

———————————————————————————————————————

Think back to your early childhood. Do you remember a nurturing relationship with your parents that included mother-and-child or father-and-child bonding? Or was your relationship distant, cold, or even traumatic? How did this affect you?

Looking for Love

I remember one time when I was little—preschool age—and visiting my dad for the weekend. Visits were sporadic; and every time, he lived in a different place. There was not much supervision (and by *not much* I mean "none"), and this particular afternoon I wandered around the neighborhood with a neighbor girl. Since I had no idea where I was, I followed her lead.

At some point we heard some music coming from a house, so we followed the sound down a driveway and realized it was coming from a basement. We opened the screen door and boldly let ourselves in. We walked down the stairs where we found some middle-aged men sporting beards and flannel button-down shirts playing their musical instruments while singing. They were jamming out a very popular hit that I recognized from the radio, "Looking for Love" by Waylon Jennings. The men kept playing, we watched for a bit, then grew bored and left, moving on to find our next neighborhood adventure.

As this song says, many of us look for love in the wrong places. We get involved in destructive relationships and pursue toxic friendships.

If we grew up in a home where we did not receive unconditional love, we might spend a lifetime looking for it—in all the wrong places. Maybe you're unsure of what conditional love looks like. Consider these descriptions:

- Your parents set an impossible standard, and you felt as if you had to earn their love.
- Your parents loved you when it was convenient for them, but then quickly dismissed you when a better offer came along.
- Your parents tried to mold you into a mini version of themselves.
- Your parents played favorites between you and your siblings.

When we don't receive adequate, healthy, unconditional love from our parents, we go looking for it in all the wrong places. That's why children from divorced homes generally have a more difficult time developing peer relationships than children raised in intact homes.[9] Children raised in divorced families are also at greater risk of becoming hostile toward adults because they don't know how to process or voice their feelings regarding the divorce. They experience higher levels of anxiety and sometimes withdraw from family, friends, and activities they enjoy.

For children of divorce, time does not heal all wounds. If you are one of these children, you are probably nodding your head right now. All the stress, anxiety, and loneliness a child feels might stay with them into their teens and young adulthood, causing them to eagerly leave home to get married, cohabit, or live independently before they are emotionally or mentally mature enough to handle these responsibilities.[10] They are not running boldly into their future . . . they are running away from their past.[11]

Divorce is not a stand-alone event but often contains a host of other vile issues that contribute to the downfall of the marriage. If you were raised in a home where alcohol, drugs, or abuse were as common as Fourth of July fireworks, then you know the long-term damage these traumas can cause. For example, children raised in alcoholic families have trouble forming romantic relationships.[12] Research also shows that "physical, emotional or sexual abuse in childhood can have lifelong effects. In relationships, survivors of early trauma often struggle with social isolation, attachment problems, and an inability to trust."[13]

This might resonate with you if you engaged in an unhealthy relationship (or a series of relationships) in your teens or early adulthood that you know was simply a way of seeking love and affection that you did not receive at home. If this describes you, it helps to understand that your attraction to a toxic person or situation was a subconscious need to fill an emotional void. You were looking for love in all the wrong places because you never received it in the right places from the right people.

As you begin to understand your choices and actions, choose to embrace grace. The motivation behind your choices was pain, loneliness, or abuse, and God knows that. Confess your part to Him, then receive His forgiveness. You can't undo the past, but you can move forward into a healthier future.

In what ways have you gone looking for love in all the wrong places?

If this is a pattern of behavior, what can you do to break this cycle?

Depression

Depression is another reason we have trouble connecting intimately with our husbands. As I mentioned earlier, sometimes women who come from dysfunctional families struggle with depression because of repressed memories or post-traumatic stress disorder (PTSD). Maybe you held it all together during the chaos of living at home, but now that you have moved out and are past the crisis, you've shut down mentally or physically, or both. This isn't your fault; it's your body's way of coping with a stressful, traumatic situation that was too scary and overwhelming for your brain to process during the crisis.

You may also be dealing with changing hormones if you have recently given birth or if you are starting to age. You should pause to consider all the factors that lead to depression. While some anti-depressants can lower a woman's desire for intimacy, depression itself builds a wall between a wife and her husband. If you think you are depressed, talk to a friend, a counselor, or a doctor, and find the right combination of counseling and medication. This, along with support from your friends and family, will lead you out of the darkness and into the light.

Maybe you are just now realizing the effect your past has on your present views of sex. Maybe you are just now coming to terms with the impact of past sexual or physical abuse. Maybe you're just beginning to understand the unhealthy view of sex that was instilled in you at a young age. Maybe you're just beginning to release feelings of guilt over a tainted past or sexual sin. Maybe you've never told anyone about the pain you endured, or maybe you did and it wasn't received the way you'd hoped.

If any of these situations sound familiar, I encourage you to seek help. God created sex as a gift, and He longs for you to enjoy it within the context of a healthy marriage. Seek wisdom from a mentor or a counselor who can help you walk through your past and find hope and healing for your future.

Also, take time to pray through your childhood memories. If you have early memories regarding sex that might be tainting your current views of sex and painting a less than God-honoring picture, bring those into the light. Sit with them. Process them. Seek a trusted friend, mentor, or even a counselor who can help you process what you're learning. You don't need to walk this road alone. This step is a huge piece of the puzzle in achieving emotional health and strength in your personal life and marriage. So don't rush through the process.

Strengthening Your Roots

1. How were you first exposed to the idea of sex?

How did it impact your views on sex while you were growing up?

How does it impact your views on sex today?

2. What trouble with connecting intimately with your husband have you had?

3. Based on what you've learned in this chapter, why do you think you struggle in this area?

What step(s) can you take to connect with your husband?

12

LIVING WATER

Connecting Through the Spirit

I began experiencing migraines when I was ten years old. In some seasons of my life they are not too severe, but in others they are unbearable. A couple years into our marriage I suffered a migraine that lasted twenty-four hours a day, seven days a week, for six months straight. Not one day of relief. It was excruciating, frustrating, and miserable.

But I received the sweetest gift because of that dark time: Brandon's intense prayers prayed over me. He lay in bed next to me—always in a dark, quiet room—and rubbed my temples day after day and night after night. He prayed for healing and relief. He prayed for strength to endure the bad days. He prayed for mercy. He prayed for faith.

But he also voiced gratitude. He gave thanks for the blessings of family and friends and meals left on our front porch. He gave thanks for medical care and doctors and life. And then he gave thanks for me—the helpless, drain of a wife who couldn't smile, couldn't laugh, couldn't go to the grocery store, or cook, or go to a restaurant or church; a wife who had quit her job and become a shell of the vibrant, talkative, long-distance running soul mate he had married just two years earlier. He gave thanks for all of that.

We prayed a lot during that season. We prayed together. We prayed separately. Unlike today, back then we were never too busy to pray. God did not answer our prayers right away. And when He finally did answer our prayers, He did not answer them the way we wanted Him to. I did not receive a miraculous, instantaneous healing; rather, I received doctors, medications, and treatment plans that helped me manage the pain. But through this journey, I grew closer to God and closer to Brandon.

There are reasons God asks us to practice spiritual disciplines. When Brandon prayed for me, he connected us to our heavenly Father, and by doing so it transformed us both. When we plant a seed, we hope it will someday look less like a seed and more like a gorgeous, blooming rose. Likewise, God wants us to look less like ourselves and more like Jesus.

Though the world tells us to live out our dreams, take care of number one, and satisfy our every craving, God tells us to live out the Great Commission (Matt. 28:19), care for the widows and orphans (James 1:27), and satisfy our deepest desires through knowing His Son (John 4:14).

To look like Jesus, we have to take the focus off ourselves and keep our eyes fixed on God—something that takes practice. This constant connection with our heavenly Father helps us maintain a humble posture and the right order within creation.

And here's a bonus. Practicing spiritual disciplines not only connects us with God but also, when practiced within marriage, brings us closer to our spouses.

Implementing Spiritual Disciplines

As I mentioned in chapter 10, just like multicolored fall leaves drifting to the ground, we are all unique in the body of Christ. God knows this because He created each one of us. And because He created us each uniquely, He graciously provides a way for each of us to seek Him, relate to Him, and know Him.

Some people connect through nature, some through liturgical tradition, and others through Bible study. One night while teaching this lesson, I made the observation that I'm very service-oriented, and I connect with God through doing. "I'm passionate about people and serving others," I said.

Brandon looked at me with that you're-half-crazy look and said, "You're passionate about causes, not people."

"I take offense to that," I objected. "I'm raising five little people." Embarrassingly, he was right though. I often care more about principle than people. I fight for causes, not compassion. I'm vocal about my relationship with Jesus, never shying away from telling others about the night-and-day difference He's made in my life.

Brandon, on the other hand, is a feeler. He's empathetic, sensitive, and intuitive. Then he goes a step further and neglects his own demanding schedule to help a friend in need. His relationship with Jesus is quiet. He prefers one-on-one mentoring to sharing his life story in a book (sorry, honey).

Various disciplines appeal to different people depending on temperament, personality, background, life experiences, and season of life. I like to study God's Word, journal, serve, and read books by contemporary Christian authors before dissecting each chapter with close friends. Brandon prefers short daily devotionals, fasting, and prayer. Fortunately, God created spiritual disciplines that would help everyone connect with Him. Consider these ways in which you can connect with God:

- *Fasting*—abstaining from food or other activities (I'm talking to you, social media fans!) for a certain period of time in order to focus more on God and spend time in prayer
- *Memorizing Scripture*—committing Scripture to memory so it can quickly come to mind to comfort, correct, and encourage
- *Observing silence*—spending time unplugged, in solitude and quiet, to be alone with God (while praying, reading, journaling, meditating, or worshipping)
- *Praying*—communicating with God (not only talking to Him but hearing what He has to say)
- *Sabbath rest*—setting time aside each week to worship God, celebrate what He has done, and rest in order to be productive and energized the rest of the week
- *Seeking solitude*—retreating to a place of seclusion to practice other spiritual disciplines without distractions
- *Serving*—helping others or providing for a need, not out of obligation but to show others Christ's love
- *Studying the Bible*—reading, analyzing, observing, and interpreting

Scripture and the truths God reveals through His written Word so
we may apply those truths to our lives

- *Tithing*—giving a portion of your income (most churches believe
  Scripture advocates for 10 percent) to the church as an offering of
  worship, thanksgiving, and faith in God's provision

Which of these disciplines do you currently practice, and how do they draw you
closer to Jesus?

Which of these disciplines do you want to incorporate into your spiritual life? Why?

If you're still not sure how to connect with God, a great place to start is
the book *The Spirit of the Disciplines* by Dallas Willard. Growing spiritually
as a couple depends on growing spiritually as an individual. Scripture reads,
"Blessed are those who hunger and thirst for righteousness, for they will be
filled" (Matt. 5:6). If we, as individuals, strive to look more like our Savior,
chances are our marriages will reflect the kingdom, and our family trees will
stand tall and grand in an otherwise sparse landscape.

Develop a Plan

In her book *The Surprising Secrets of Highly Happy Marriages*, Shaunti Feldhahn conducts research on marriage and specifically on what creates a happy marriage. She asserts that 53 percent of "very happy couples" agree with the statement, "God is at the center of our marriage" as compared to 7 percent of "struggling couples." Feldhahn interviewed hundreds of people outside the church and expected them not to believe in God. However, they repeatedly mentioned God and pointed to Him as the source of their happiness in marriage. "Relying on Him gave them the security of knowing that Someone higher than themselves was in control—Someone on whom they could rely for the selflessness needed to put the other person first and create a great marriage. Not only that, but the knowledge that their spouses were looking to God for fulfillment—rather than to them—took the pressure off trying to provide something that, in the end, only God can really provide."[1] The psalmist was correct when he wrote, "Unless the Lord builds the house, the builders labor in vain" (Ps. 127:1).

With so many outside forces competing for our attention, how do we bring God into the center of our marriage? The daily demands of work, family, friends, committee meetings, community service, and—dare I say it?—church pull our attention away from the glue that binds a marriage together. The hustle and bustle of life takes over, and without even realizing it, we force the God of the universe to become a spectator of our lives instead of allowing Him to be at the center of our lives.

Every Sunday night I make our meal plan for the week. This meal plan determines my grocery list. If I don't go to the grocery store, I don't buy food to cook for my family. When I don't buy food to cook for my family, dinner is a chaotic free-for-all resulting in whiney children, a confused husband, and an unhealthy smorgasbord of corn dogs, canned green beans, and Fritos. The chaos of trying to pull a last-minute edible rabbit out of my hat for dinner causes stress for everyone. I feel guilty, overwhelmed, and short-tempered. No one is connecting—we are all just surviving.

Just as I must discipline myself to create a meal plan, I must stay disciplined in my spiritual life. You might think strategizing for spiritual growth sounds mechanical or shallow, but intentionality is the best insurance for success. We plan a doctor's visit to ensure our physical health. We plan our coffee dates with friends to ensure our emotional health. In the same way, we should implement spiritual disciplines to ensure our spiritual health.

Determine your peak time of day and schedule time with God. Whether you're a morning person, a night owl, a stay-at-home mom who can spend time in the Word during your kids' nap, or a working woman who can read the Bible on her lunch hour, take advantage of your free time no matter how limited. Remember that if you did not grow up in a family where people read the Bible regularly, memorized Scripture, observed the Sabbath, prayed consistently, fasted, or engaged in any other type of spiritual discipline, then these practices might not come naturally to you; in fact, they might feel foreign or uncomfortable.

My advice is to start small. Add one discipline at a time. Once one discipline feels automatic and natural, add another discipline. When it also feels like a natural part of your life, add another and continue your journey.

What prevents you from incorporating spiritual disciplines into your life? Is it a lack of planning? Or something else?

Learn Not to Exasperate Your . . . Spouse?

The apostle Paul warned the parents in Ephesus and then later in Colossae against exasperating their children. "Fathers: don't infuriate your children, so their hearts won't harbor resentment and become discouraged" (Col. 3:21 VOICE).

This advice is beneficial when we think about how we connect with God. We shouldn't force our children to spend time with God the same way we spend time with our Creator because our children might be wired differently than us.

For instance, I love to read and spend time studying God's Word, as does my oldest son, Carter. My daughter Clarey, on the other hand, loves art. Neither Brandon nor I are artistic. I half wonder if Clarey was switched at birth, and our pragmatic, analytical daughter who only knows how to draw stick figures is out there somewhere wondering why she is a great disappointment to her art professor "mother."

I think it's safe to assume that dissecting sections of Scripture is not how Clarey will connect with God. However, prepare your eyes for a masterpiece if I write a Bible verse on an index card and give it to Clarey along with a piece of poster board and tell her to create a picture depicting the passage using sequins, markers, glitter pens, and stickers. Not only that, she will mull over that passage every single day for a week as she puts the finishing touches on her work of art. By the end of the week she will have memorized the verse and absorbed the meaning behind the words.

Contrast her way of connecting with God with being made to sit and read the Bible for twenty minutes every day. The first method will capture her heart and her mind; it will draw her into the story of her Savior. The second will frustrate her, bore her, and cause resentment to well up inside her because it doesn't fit with the way she was designed to encounter God.

Just like we do with our children, sometimes we try to force our spouses to connect with God the same way we connect with Him. Brandon chooses to read devotionals, while I love concordances and lexicons and using five different Bible translations. We might not read Scripture the same way, but we give each other permission to experience God in our own ways, according to our own needs. Sometimes giving each other space and time to pursue God individually is not convenient, but it is respectful, and it allows us to grow in marriage and in our spiritual intimacy with one another and with God. The beauty of the journey is that when God speaks to us individually, we have something to share with the other person.

How are you and your spouse giving each other freedom to pursue God in your unique ways?

Trust Your Good, Good Father

No matter what spiritual disciplines we practice, the end goal is to connect with our heavenly Father. Recently our church's worship team led the congregation in a song called, "Good, Good Father" by Chris Tomlin. If you haven't already, I highly recommend you listen to the song.

I admit that for many months when our congregation sang this song, I remained silent with tears welling up in my eyes. While everyone around me worshipped, some with arms raised to honor our Savior, I stood paralyzed, pondering many questions:

- Do I really believe God is a good, good Father?
- Do I believe all of His ways are perfect, as the song asserts?
- If so, do I believe the sin and dysfunction in my life were perfect?
- Do I believe the emotional scars I bear today are perfect?
- Do I believe that when God allowed me to grow up without a dad, God's ways were perfect?

I stood and listened to the hundreds of voices around me singing as I wondered what *good* and *perfect* even meant. Maybe you can relate. If you had a parent who was less than good, it might be challenging to relate to a heavenly Father who is good, perfect, and loving. If you never felt unconditional love from your mom or dad, you might find it difficult to feel or even trust the pure, sacred love your heavenly Father offers you.

When we doubt God's love for us, we must return to the truth we know, which is that God loves us so much He sacrificed His only Son for us—for *us* (John 3:16)! I don't know a parent or friend or anyone in the world who would do such a thing, but God did it. He did it for me, and He did it for you.

We might also wonder if God is strong enough to save us. "Can He really rescue me?" you might wonder. "My grandparents, teachers, caseworkers—no one could save me from my abusive parents. How is He going to save me now?"

First, we must remember that it was not God who committed offenses against us, nor did He give other people permission to do so—it was sinful, fallen people who acted heinously. God is only responsible for giving them the free will to do so.

The prayers you voiced while hiding in your closet, while eating dinner all alone, while waiting for the fighting to subside might not have been answered the way you wanted. But rest assured, God saved you. You know this because you are reading this book. You persevered. You survived. You triumphed. The psalmist writes, "In their distress, they called out to the Eternal, and He saved them from their misery" (Ps. 107:28 voice).

Eventually, after many months of singing "Good, Good Father" and after spending lots of time in prayer, I landed on these truths:

- God is good.
- God is love.
- God loves me.
- God's heart breaks when my heart breaks.
- This world and the people in it are imperfect.
- I am imperfect.
- God, however, is perfect.

If we want to connect with God, we must accept the truth that He *is* a good Father. We often assume God is absent when we struggle, that somehow He checks out or watches with a stoic persona until our trial is over. Yet nothing could be further from the truth. Like a loving parent watching his child, God longs to comfort us when we hurt. When we cry, God feels our suffering. God created us, watched over us, sent His Son to die on our behalf, and then sent the Holy Spirit to intercede on our behalf. Now that is a good, good Father whom we can trust!

Do you believe God is a good, good Father? Explain.

Strengthening Your Roots

1. Is it difficult for you to believe that all of God's ways are perfect? Explain.

2. Which spiritual disciplines are you currently practicing to help you draw closer to God?

3. Which spiritual disciplines would you like to incorporate into your life and why? How do you plan on making that happen?

4. In what ways do you encourage your spouse on a spiritual level? In what ways do you exasperate your spouse on a spiritual level?

GRACEFUL GROWTH

Living Out Forgiveness

As children from dysfunctional families, we often grow up struggling with the issue of forgiveness. Seeds of hurt, betrayal, and pain planted in our early years continue to reap a harvest as we mature. Confusion, bitterness, and disappointment prevent our carefully sown seeds of mercy and understanding from taking root. One of these scenarios may sound familiar:

- You longed for your parents' approval but never received it. Even today you sense their disapproval of your life choices.
- Your mom chose men more than she chose you. Now that you're grown, she refuses to acknowledge the choices she made.
- Your dad spent more time at work than he did at home, and you can never get those years back.
- Your parents invested more time in the church than they did in you.
- Your parents' love for you was based on your achievement, yet no awards or grades were ever enough to earn their love.
- Your extended family ignored the abuse in your home while you suffered in silence.

Now you are an adult. The wounds have healed, but the scars remain. You know God's Word in your head, but your heart still aches. Each of us must find our own path to forgiveness, but ultimately the goal is for all of us to move from a place of pain to a place of peace, from indifference to compassion.

After years of family dysfunction, my fellow broken branch Marissa endured a painful wedding day. Not only did her alcoholic mom arrive drunk, but she proceeded to pick a fight and slap Marissa at the reception in front of all the guests. Asking a daughter to forgive her mother for ruining one of the most sacred and special days in her life seems almost impossible. For Marissa, this act of forgiveness almost was. But with God's help, forgiveness and healing did arrive, even years after harboring deep hatred and resentment.

Marissa ✿ I didn't always pray for God to take away my anger and resentment, but I started to realize the stronghold it had on my life and my marriage and how deeply it was affecting my husband. We both felt angry, and that's just not who we are. I was hung up on the fact that she was my mother, and I had to figure out what our relationship should look like now that I was an adult and a wife, and had my own family.

I asked myself, "What is going to come of me holding on to the past? Will it change her?" No. "Will it change what happened?" No. "Will it heal me?" No. At that point, I knew I had to be done with my mom. So, through much prayer, I let her go. I released her to the Lord and decided that I needed to pray for her—for healing from her illness. I haven't been around my mom in over three years, but I have fully forgiven her.

My heart doesn't long for her anymore. God has placed women in my life to serve as mentors and mothers to guide me through my first year of marriage, to love me, to care for me, and to let me confide in them. He replaced that void in a way I could never have imagined. Through forgiveness I have been freed to fully belong to my husband and to invest in our marriage.

Another fellow broken branch, Martha Kate, experienced her own journey of suffering and forgiveness. Martha Kate battled an eating disorder for twelve years. The reasons contributing to her disease are many, but she knows her complicated relationship with her parents, especially her mom, played a large role. When it came to recovering from her illness, Martha Kate knew she needed to pursue forgiveness. She doesn't excuse her parents' behavior, but she does recognize that she is herself a sinner, just as they are. "For all have sinned and fall short of the glory of God," Romans 3:23 teaches. This truth helps bring her freedom from her disease and from the grips of anger and unforgiveness.

> *Martha Kate* ❀ I realized that my parents did the best they could with the tools they were given. That truth has been very freeing. I also realized that blaming my parents wouldn't lead to my healing; it would only lead to bitterness. I think understanding that we are sinners, just as our parents are, is so freeing and humbling.

How has your journey to forgive been similar to these women's? How has it been different?

What would you like your road to forgiveness to look like?

The Definition of Forgiveness

Too many people get tangled up in the twisted thorny vine of semantics and misconceptions about forgiveness. So let's clear up any confusion and clearly define forgiveness.

Forgiveness is an act of strength, as well as many other things:

- A biblically mandated action
- A conscious choice on the part of the offended
- Part of the emotional, mental, and spiritual healing process
- A sign of emotional, mental, and spiritual strength and maturity
- A one-sided practice; the person forgiving does not need permission from the offender to forgive
- Letting go of the need for revenge
- Letting go of bitterness, hatred, and resentment

Despite what you might have heard or believed in the past, please know that forgiveness is *not* the following things:

- Giving the offender a free pass
- Forgetting the offense itself
- A sign of weakness in the person offering forgiveness
- Pretending the offense never occurred
- Condoning the offender's past behavior
- Enabling wrong behavior
- A one-time event
- Reconciliation, which requires cooperation from two people

God calls us to forgive for many reasons. First, because we are all transgressors. Yes, we like to focus on our own pain: *Look what she did to me! Look how he hurt me!* But we are sinners too. Wise King Solomon reminds us of our own imperfections: "There is not a righteous person on earth who *always* does good and never sins" (Eccl. 7:20 voice).

Second, we must forgive because God first forgave us. "For God so loved the world that he gave his one and only Son, that whoever believes in him shall not perish but have eternal life" (John 3:16). If someone who is absolutely perfect can forgive imperfect me, surely I can humble myself and forgive others.

Finally, God knows that forgiveness frees us from negative emotions such as hatred and bitterness. "Hatred stirs up conflict, but love covers over all wrongs" (Prov. 10:12).

And while forgiving someone repeatedly might feel exhausting, according to Jesus there is no end to how many times we must forgive. Peter came to Jesus and asked, "'Lord, how often should I forgive someone who sins against me? Seven times?' 'No, not seven times,' Jesus replied, 'but seventy times seven!'" (Matt. 18:21–22 NLT).

In the book *Boundaries*, Henry Cloud and John Townsend write,

When you refuse to forgive someone, you still want something from that person, and even if it is revenge that you want, it *keeps you tied to him forever.*

Refusing to forgive a family member is one of the main reasons people are stuck for years, unable to separate from their dysfunctional families. They still want something from them. . . .

If you do not forgive, you are demanding something your offender does not choose to give, even if it is only confession of what he did. This "ties" him to you and ruins boundaries. Let the dysfunctional family you came from go. Cut it loose, and you will be free.[1]

What misconceptions about forgiveness have you clung to?

Working Toward Forgiveness

After my mom's second divorce, I processed the loss of my stepdad—and the loss of a dream. I thought he was going to adopt me. I thought we would be a forever family. I thought we would live out our fairy tale and live happily ever after. But volatile arguments, abuse, and adultery turned my fairy tale into a reality tale. I held on to so much anger toward my stepdad that forgiveness seemed impossible.

As a new believer, I attended every Bible study and Christian ministry my school offered. After living the majority of my life without a Savior, I longed to soak up spiritual truth and gain a deeper understanding of the gospel. Day by day, my spiritual roots grew deeper and stronger. And, let's be honest, if a cute boy was around, I saw no harm in sitting together, as long as we left room for the Holy Spirit.

During this time a few Scriptures came to the forefront of my consciousness, the first being the parable of the unmerciful servant. If you have not read this story, let me give you the condensed version.

The first servant—let's call him Big Debtor—finds himself owing more money to his king than he could ever repay in a lifetime. Let's estimate around seven trillion dollars, just for fun. Big Debtor begs the king for mercy. Surprisingly, the king forgives the debt.

After receiving the biggest get-out-of-jail-free card in history, Big Debtor meets up with another servant—Little Debtor. Little Debtor owes Big Debtor about a day's wage. No big deal. Little Debtor begs Big Debtor for mercy. (Déjà vu.) But Big Debtor throws Little Debtor in jail. (Hypocrite.)

The king hears about Big Debtor's mockery. "In anger his master handed him over to the jailers to be tortured, until he should pay back all he owed" (Matt. 18:34). Jesus tells the people, "This is how my heavenly Father will treat each of you unless you forgive your brother or sister from your heart" (v. 35).

God used this Scripture to show me that Jesus, my King, had forgiven me, yet I refused to extend this same forgiveness toward my stepdad. I harbored so much resentment and bitterness toward him, even though I was the only person suffering as a result. I had a choice. I could respond like the king and experience freedom or respond like Big Debtor and feel tortured and angry for the rest of my life. Fortunately, God helped me release my pride so I could choose forgiveness and freedom.

> *Leslie* ❈ I struggled for many years, but the Lord brought me to a place where I was finally able to forgive past hurts, the most painful of which came from my relationship with my mother. God has used those hurts to bring me closer to Him and to my husband.

Who is God calling you to forgive? What has held you back from forgiving that person before now? Explain.

A Biblical Example of Forgiveness

The biblical story of Joseph also shaped my understanding of forgiveness and reconciliation. If you have time, read Genesis 37–45. The following chart supplies the highlights from Joseph's life.

Favored	Gen. 37	Joseph is the youngest of twelve brothers and favored by their father Jacob. Joseph uses poor judgment by making sure his brothers know this fact. (Sibling rivalry at its finest!)
Sold	Gen. 37	Out of jealousy, Joseph's brothers plan to kill him. Then they decide to have mercy on him and "just" sell him into slavery.
Imprisoned	Gen. 39	Potiphar, one of Pharaoh's officials, buys Joseph. Potiphar's wife falsely accuses Joseph of rape, and he is sent to prison. (Tough day at the office, Joseph.)
Gifted	Gen. 40–41	While imprisoned, Joseph interprets a dream for Pharaoh's former cupbearer. Upon release from jail, the cupbearer promises to remember Joseph, but he forgets his promise (ugh). Two years later, the cupbearer finally remembers Joseph, and Joseph interprets Pharaoh's dream regarding seven years of harvest and seven years of famine in Egypt.
Elevated	Gen. 41	Joseph is released from prison and put in charge of Egypt's food supply. Joseph goes to work for Pharaoh. (Score!)
Approached	Gen. 42	Joseph's brothers travel from Canaan to Egypt to escape famine in their own land. They don't recognize Joseph, but he recognizes them. (Someone sold into slavery doesn't quickly forget his betrayers.)
Reunited	Gen. 43	Joseph is reunited with his brothers, although they still don't know Joseph's true identity. (Get a clue, people!)
Framed	Gen. 44	Joseph sets his brothers up for the possibility of losing their freedom, just as he lost his own so many years ago.
Forgiven	Gen. 45	Joseph reveals his identity to his brothers and sends for his father. His brothers apologize and repent, and Joseph forgives them. (And this is why people will forever remember Joseph, and not me. What an example for all of us to follow!)
Reconciled	Gen. 50	Joseph once again extends forgiveness to his brothers and even vows to care for his brothers' children.

No doubt Joseph dealt with issues of forgiveness in his life. Which is why the humble words he spoke to his brothers have always astounded me. "'You intended to harm me, but God intended it for good to accomplish what is now being done, the saving of many lives. So then, don't be afraid. I will provide for you and your children.' And he reassured them and spoke kindly to them" (Gen. 50:20–21). I wonder if I could say those same words to someone who had betrayed me.

Which part of Joseph's story stands out most to you?

How does Joseph's story apply to your own story in relation to forgiveness?

Forgiveness and Grace

A few years ago, Brandon and I rented the Academy Award–winning movie *12 Years a Slave*. (When you have five little ones, you tend to see movies long after the red carpet is rolled up and everyone has gone home.)

I knew the movie received rave reviews, and I couldn't wait to see the powerhouse performance by Academy Award–winner Lupita Nyong'o.

Obviously I had studied slavery in school and seen other movies on the subject, but no textbook lesson or *E! News* interview prepared me for the brutality I witnessed in this movie. I felt physically nauseous for days after

I saw it. I could barely eat and would cry just driving around town while running errands.

"Am I the only one who has seen this movie!" I half thought, half shouted in my car. If everyone saw what I had just seen, there should be a louder uproar. A bigger outrage. "Why," I wondered, "is everyone carrying on with life as if nothing had happened?"

To this day I can't get the images out of my mind. My heart aches for what the slaves endured. After all, they are not merely characters. The movie is based on a true story about real people who lived and died and suffered and cried and wept and moaned.

I admit I will never fully grasp the concept of slavery. I am just a little white girl, born in the 1970s, raised on *Garbage Pail Kids* and *New Kids on the Block* in the 1980s, and now living in the new millennium, enjoying Starbucks and free Wi-Fi everywhere I go. I know nothing about oppression and poverty.

What I do know is that movies like *12 Years a Slave* educate me. I used to think slavery was just hard labor without pay. *Forgive me, Father, for I know not what I think.* From what my feeble mind now grasps, slavery is evil personified. It is oppression and ignorance. It is humiliation, separation, abuse, fear, degradation, and perversion. It is one of the most horrific practices in our country's history and our children's most disgraceful legacy. It has created broken branches that our country will forever be trying to mend.

At one point in the movie the young, beautiful slave named Patsy, played by Nyong'o, begs another slave named Solomon to kill her in the river. When he asks her why she wants to die she tells him, "There is no comfort for me in this life."

No comfort. No hope. No joy. Nothing but pain, fear, sadness, torture, and loneliness twenty-four hours a day, seven days a week, three hundred sixty-five days a year for the rest of her life—that is slavery.

I wonder if you felt enslaved—or trapped—in your own dysfunctional family. Maybe you can relate to Patsy in that you grew up feeling there was no comfort for you. Maybe you grew up feeling afraid, hopeless, or humiliated.

After watching such a tragedy play out for three long hours, I marveled even more at what Joseph endured. No doubt he withstood comfortless, hopeless, humiliating days while sitting in his cold, dark, lonely cell.

Even so, years later, Joseph the slave not only forgave those who had sold him into slavery, but as Scripture tells us, he also spoke kindly and generously to them. He saved their lives. He chose to repair his broken branches instead of tearing up his roots by seeking revenge. Only grace makes such a thing possible.

We see grace play a role in the lives of other biblical heroes as well. After David and Bathsheba committed adultery, the son they conceived died. Yet God gave them another son—King Solomon. That is grace. Saul preached against the gospel and killed countless Christians, yet went on to become the greatest evangelist of our time. That is grace. Jesus committed no sin, yet died a humiliating, horrific death on the cross to save us from our sins. That is grace.

Grace is defined as undeserved favor; it is offering something to someone who does not deserve it. How has God extended grace to you?

How can you apply grace to someone in your life?

Moving from Forgiveness to Reconciliation

It takes only one person to forgive but two people to reconcile. If the following guidelines have been fulfilled, then you can consider reconciliation:

- Forgiveness has been offered by the offender and accepted by the offended.
- Both people seek reconciliation.
- Both people welcome accountability.
- The offender stops the hurtful behavior.
- The offender accepts responsibility for the hurt he or she caused.
- The offender makes restitution where necessary.

Reconciliation is a messy, grueling process that is mentally, emotionally, and spiritually draining. Yet it can be a healing, sanctifying, and freeing experience that draws you closer to one another and to your Savior.

Catherine ❀ I think I have mostly forgiven my mom, but there are moments when it's clear I still struggle. When my mom died, it took away a lot of the anger I felt for her (death has a way of changing your perspective) and made me long to have her back, warts and all. There are times when I think back and feel really sad about my childhood, but my childhood made me who I am now, and I can appreciate that. I think all my experiences growing up have made my marriage stronger.

With whom is God calling you to seek reconciliation?

How will you pursue reconciliation with that person?

Strengthening Your Roots

1. List all the people Joseph needed to forgive in his life. His brothers are the obvious people, but who else wronged him? Next to each name, list the person's offense against Joseph.

2. What about himself? Do you think Joseph needed to forgive himself for anything? Explain.

3. How can you apply Joseph's example of forgiveness and grace to your family of origin?

4. Have you taken the time to work through forgiveness toward members of your family? Others? Take time to fill out the chart in appendix D. (A sample chart is provided there to help you get started.) If you want to make copies of the chart so you can add to it beyond your time in this book, please feel free to do so. This chart is meant to be a lifelong tool that will help you progress through forgiveness and determine if reconciliation is right for you.

PART THREE

THE FUTURE

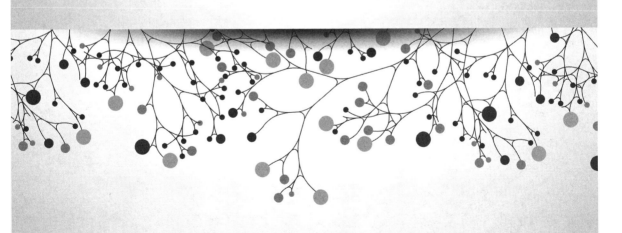

14

HEALTHY SOIL FOR GROWTH

Helping Your Husband Understand You

As a wife, you long to be loved and treasured, but maybe you need more than love as you process your past. Maybe you want your husband to also offer you understanding and empathy. Maybe you want him to walk bravely into your past and not fear the things that he finds. Invite your husband to listen as you read parts of this chapter aloud to him. If he's reluctant, introduce the concepts or questions into conversation—slowly and gently.

If you long for a deep, emotional connection with your husband, here are some key things you might want from him. Don't be afraid to voice these desires to your husband:

- I need you to support me as I process my past.
- I want you to love me selflessly in both the present and the future. (Then describe what that looks like to you.)
- I want you to understand my pain and my fears.
- I need you to understand why marriage and family are so important to me, yet at the same time relationships are so difficult for me.

Nurturing and understanding your soul is like mixing nutrients into the soil to help a plant grow. Remember that you endured more than the average person. You are strong, yet fragile. You are independent, yet you long for your husband to care for you. It's OK to admit you are complex, yet worth every bit of love and energy your husband pours into you.

Which Kind of Husband Did You Marry?

Odds are you grew up without a godly man leading your family—no husband doting on his wife, no man taking your mom on date nights, no father praying at dinner, no daddy leading nighttime devotionals, no dad comforting you when you got cut from the volleyball team, no father telling you that you looked beautiful on prom night, and no father of the bride walking you down the aisle. So now that you're married, your husband's character and how he leads your family means a great deal to you.

> *Ellie* ❋ The character of a man sets the foundation for how he will lead his family and love his wife and children. A lack of character equals a lack of leadership.

You had no role model of a healthy husband (or of a healthy father), yet somehow you found your way to your husband. Women from dysfunctional families generally date and marry someone who fits one of the following profiles (whether it is a conscious or subconscious choice). Read the list below and think about which one describes your husband.

- *Mr. Perfect.* You were so determined to mend your broken branches that you looked for someone who acted completely differently from anyone in your family. When the honeymoon period was over and reality hit, you were so resolved to be the perfect wife with the perfect husband and create the perfect family—the exact opposite of what you knew growing up—that you tried to fit your husband into a perfect mold. This ideal is so unattainable that any husband, including yours, will eventually fail—not because he doesn't try to please you or he doesn't love you, but because he is human. He can never live up to your unrealistic expectations so he will always disappoint you.
- *Mr. Twin.* You wanted to overcome your past, but the dysfunction and chaos was all you knew, so you married someone exactly like your father. (People often gravitate toward the familiar even when

the familiar is destructive.) In some ways this familiarity comforts you because you know how to handle your father; therefore, you know how to handle your husband. On the other hand, you feel deep regret. You wanted to change your family tree, but now you realize you are only deepening its destructive roots.

- *Mr. Opposite.* Your father hurt and disappointed you, so you married someone with all the opposite qualities. Even so, your past is painful, and your husband should be patient with you as you process it.

- *Mr. Media.* You grew up fatherless, so your idea of a perfect husband and father of your children came from a hodgepodge of movies and television shows (because those are so reliable), and now you're in it to win it, determined to make your marriage work. Unfortunately, this marriage thing isn't as easy as all those romantic comedies make it seem. Suddenly, there is no audience laughing, no wild make-up sex, and the problems aren't solved in thirty minutes.

Which husband looks most like your husband?

Why did you gravitate toward this type of husband?

How has it affected your marriage?

Marissa ✻ Throughout my childhood, the adults who were supposed to love, nurture, protect, and care for me didn't. They constantly let me down, and that filled me with insecurity and anxiety.
In my teenage years the insecurity was so frightful that I over-
compensated by cutting ties and building walls to keep people at a
distance. This helped me protect myself from disappointment and
vacant promises.

Accepting my husband and allowing him to take control and
take care of me has been the most difficult part of our marriage.
Although I've placed boundaries between me and my family of
origin, pain and a weight still burden my heart when something
happens with them. When I hurt, my husband hurts. And it makes
me angry that my family affects him in that way. But he always
reminds me that he knew about my family when he chose me. It
took me a while to realize the beauty in that.

The Lord aligned my path with that of a man who is graceful,
quietly assertive, and forgiving, and who comes from a background
completely opposite to mine. At first, I felt a lot of resentment that
his parents have been married for over thirty years and that he gets
along with his sisters so well. But now I see that God's purpose
and intention was to give me a family that is truly loving, caring,
and constant—to make such a family part of my story and legacy.
I couldn't have imagined such a gift in my wildest dreams. To God
be all the glory.

Your Husband's Spiritual Life

Husbands have a tough job; they must stay grounded in their faith, lead their
wives well, and reassure their wives of safety. These are not easy tasks.

Creating a healthy marriage starts with a husband's relationship with
Jesus. If his spiritual life is stable, he'll be able to lend stability to his relationships with his wife and children. Just as Jesus willingly sacrificed Himself
for us—for the church—God wants husbands to gladly sacrifice their own
desires for their wives' needs and wants. This includes small sacrifices such

as making the bed or watching the kids so his wife can have coffee with a friend, as well as bigger things such as supporting her dreams at the cost of his own. All of this is driven by a husband's intimate relationship with Jesus. "Husbands, love your wives, just as Christ loved the church and gave himself up for her" (Eph. 5:25).

Although we sometimes wish we could (and sometimes try), we cannot control our husbands' spiritual lives. But if you want a healthy spiritual connection with your husband, you can do the following:

- Maintain your own healthy relationship with God through the various disciplines we discussed in chapter 12.
- Pray for your husband.
- Ask your husband how you can pray for him.
- Ask your husband to pray *for* you, and tell him what specific prayer needs you have.
- Ask your husband to pray *with* you.
- Talk to your husband about what God is teaching you, making sure you approach him with a spirit of humility.
- Encourage your husband in his endeavors (work, hobbies, etc.).

On a scale of one to ten, how is your relationship with Jesus? (*One* means nonexistent, *five* means good but inconsistent, and *ten* means consistent and deep.) Explain.

If you chose a rating of seven or lower, what can you do to improve your relationship with Jesus?

Name one thing you can do this week to encourage your husband spiritually.

Connecting Through Conversation

In chapter 8 we discussed communication and the importance of listening. Communicating intimately—and specifically talking about your past—might be very difficult for you. On one hand, you might long for a safe place where you can pour out your deepest fears, your most painful memories, and your hopes and dreams for the future. If your husband is a good, albeit imperfect, man, you have the favorable option of talking with him. If your husband is not capable of this type of deeply personal communication, you might need to find a listening ear in your best female friend, a mentor, or a professional counselor.

> *Franny* ❀ My husband's understanding and reassurance is really important to me. I have been through a lot, and it's made me who I am. I have anxiety, and even the healing process is part of my baggage. I work on forgiving myself, and I tell my husband how grateful I am for his unconditional love. He walks with me through things that haunt me, though he's never actually stepped foot into the darkness I've seen. It is hard to know what can trigger a bad memory for me, but it is comforting to know I'm never alone.

Like Franny, you may have a husband who is your partner for the good times and the bad—who walks next to you as you relive your past, whether through nightmares that wake you in the middle of the night, memories you thought you had buried but that resurface, or feelings triggered by family gatherings. But no matter how emotionally, spiritually, and physically connected you are with your husband, he will never "step foot into the darkness" you have seen. He will never live the life you lived. He will never endure the pain you felt. But he can try to understand you.

One way he can seek to understand you is to ask you questions that draw you out. Unfortunately, he might not know what questions to ask, or he might be too uncomfortable, too nervous, or too scared to broach the subject of your past. This is where you need to give him a little nudge. Don't expect him to read your mind. Let him know what you need. If you need a safe place to process your past, tell him. If no one in your life has ever listened to you, if no one gave you permission to use your voice, this might be a scary endeavor for you. But if your husband has your best interests at heart, trust in that and don't listen to the voices of your past.

Also, make sure your husband knows you just want him to listen with the purpose of gaining an understanding. You don't need him to fix anything. Some damage has been done, and now you need empathy, not pity; patience, not frustration; and grace, not judgment.

If you still need help in starting the conversation, read the questions below. Feel free to incorporate these into a date night or a state of the union meeting. And make sure to give each other a chance to answer. That way you will both be sharing, and the conversation will not be one-sided.

- What was the best part about your childhood?
- What was something difficult about your childhood?
- What would you like to do differently in our marriage from what you saw in your parents' marriage?
- What would you like to do the same way your parents did it?
- What were holidays like in your family?
- Do you have any holiday traditions you would like to keep?
- What were mealtimes like in your family?
- What did you do on the weekends when you were growing up?
- Use three words to describe your childhood.
- Use three words to describe what you want your family to look like today.
- Do you see any healthy patterns we are repeating from your family?

- Do you see any unhealthy patterns we are repeating from your family?
- What can we do to be different from your family?

Understanding Trauma

Even though we dated more than three years before marrying, it was still a long time after marrying before Brandon could peel back my layers and see the dysfunction deep within my family tree. I kept many stories locked away.

While he will never fully grasp my history, Brandon tries. He asks questions and listens. He reflects and empathizes. He tries to get to know the child I was—as if he's meeting her for the first time—because she's made me into the woman he knows today.

Friends, if you want your husband to understand you, you have to help him learn about your history. Be patient. Help him see your world—your childhood, your family of origin, your relationships—all through your perspective, so he can understand you on a deeper level.

If you grew up in a family where domestic violence was common, you need to understand the damage incurred by your psyche so you can help your husband understand the long-term effects. Judith S. Wallerstein, author of *The Unexpected Legacy of Divorce: The 25 Year Landmark Study*, writes about a young girl being verbally insulted by her abusive father.

There's almost no way a little girl hearing this can escape internalizing the view that she's an inferior being. Moreover, the violent father is often a seductive and charming man who doesn't hesitate to court his sons and daughters in the hope of enlisting their support. This combination of power and helplessness is very appealing to a child. It has strong erotic overtones. The child internalizes the image of a man who is overpowering, needy, and appealing. She buys into and internalizes a view of herself as an inferior being who needs a strong man to hang on to because, as several of these sad young women said to me, "Without a man I am nothing." As she matures, this image is built into her expectations of men and her relationships with men. The man is supposed to hurt her and she is to remain the helpless victim.[1]

Even if they do escape at a young age, women growing up in abusive homes, suffer long-lasting effects.

- They are more likely to suffer from cardiovascular disease, chronic lung and liver disease, obesity, depression, and smoking, alcohol, and drug abuse.[2]
- More than half of people with depression and women who have tried to commit suicide were connected to traumatic childhood experiences.[3]
- Childhood trauma, such as physical and sexual abuse, also puts women at risk for psychiatric disorders, physical disease, disability, health-care costs, and adverse sexual behavior.[4]

Women who grew up in a constant state of dysfunction often live in continual panic mode, ready for disaster to strike. Whatever you endured, you knew one bad event always followed another.

Tara ✹ Because of my childhood, I had the perception that there was a big, unavoidable, unknown thing waiting out there that would cause my life and my marriage to go careening off a cliff at some point. I had no concept of being with someone for ten, twenty, thirty years or more.

All of these dismal statistics might sound disheartening. You might even wonder if a happy, committed marriage is possible. Let me assure you, it is. Our God is stronger than statistics and bigger than broken branches. He has brought you this far, and He will not leave you now.

Jesus promises us, "I have told you these things, so that in me you may have peace. In this world you will have trouble. But take heart! I have overcome the world" (John 16:33). Trials are a fact in life. We cannot avoid them. Unfortunately, some people endure more trials than others, and at an earlier age. You have shown great endurance, fortitude, resilience, and faith in living through your trials. And while I am sure you are not perfect and have made your own mistakes, the sheer fact that you are emotionally, physically, and spiritually intact is a wonder. You are a survivor and a miracle to be celebrated!

Strengthening Your Roots

1. What are your expectations in a husband? List them below, then share them with your husband.

2. What is your reaction to the statistics and facts about women raised in dysfunctional families? Do these concern you? Why or why not?

Do you see any of these effects in your life? Explain.

If your husband is a safe person, ask him if he sees any of these effects in you. If so, ask him to explain.

3. When it comes to talking about your past, what do you need from your husband? A night set aside to talk? Do you need him to ask a few leading questions? Describe what you need and then tell him so he's not left to guess.

TREE HOUSES AND FORTS

Raising the Next Generation

We recently lived in a neighborhood where our children had tons of friends, sidewalks for riding bikes, prime real estate for a lemonade stand (and lots of generous neighbors), and a community playground and pool. Sounds just like Stars Hollow from *Gilmore Girls*. If Lorelei and Rory had stopped by, I might have considered staying. But the bedrooms were tiny and our people were getting big, so it was time to house hunt.

After about two years, we found an adorable traditional home in an established neighborhood (that's Realtor speak for "old neighborhood that needs some updating"). This house had a dreamy front porch and all the criteria on our list. It even had trees—one thing our old neighborhood lacked.

With an acre of land, there were trees everywhere. The front yard greeted us with a tree for a swing. The backyard offered shade for hot, sunny days and a grand tree for a hammock. The side yard provided the perfect tree for climbing. And our younger son found lots of trees way down the hill for fort building and sword fighting and every other game boys play.

As someone who moved around a lot while growing up, I can't even tell you the number of houses I've lived in. Buying a home—this home—was about more than just real estate. It was about planting roots. It was about providing a place where our children would create memories that they would tell their children. "Remember that time Dad helped us build the fort and then let us sleep in it?" Or, "Hey, Mom, remember when you used to let me read my homework in the hammock?"

This was our place where we would plant deep roots, climb trees, swing from branches, probably break a bone or two, cry a little, laugh a lot, fight every once in a while, make up always, create memories, and pass on those memories for generations to come. Yes, we had found not only a house but a home—our dream home.

Be Prepared

The Boy Scouts' motto is "Be Prepared." I wish I had been a Boy Scout, because I was definitely not prepared for the discussion I was about to have with my children.

"Mom, who's your dad?" Clarey, who was six years old, asked one afternoon as the kids and I sat around the kitchen table. She was coloring, Carter was reading, and Campbell was cutting up scraps of paper.

"Well, you don't know him, honey." I told her, trying to act casual.

"Where does he live?" she continued, as if she were playing twenty questions.

"I don't know. I haven't seen him or talked to him since I was a little girl." I said, choosing my words carefully.

Carter chimed in. "Why not?"

"Well, you guys have a very sweet daddy." I tried to use words they would understand. "Your daddy plays with you and coaches your soccer teams and tucks you in at night. But not everyone has a daddy like that. Sometimes daddies go away. That's what my daddy did. But I don't want you to worry because your daddy will never do that." I struggled to find the balance between helping them understand my world (a world where daddies leave and life is uncertain) and their world (a world where Daddy teaches them how to ride a bike, neighborhood friends play freely, and life is secure).

"Did it make you sad?" Campbell, our deep thinker, asked. "You know, when your dad went away?"

"I don't remember being sad," I answered. "I was so little that I didn't really think about it. It just always was." And then I turned the subject to more important matters like what kind of ice cream I should buy at the store. The brief interaction was all I could handle for one day.

When I became a mom, I never prepared myself for answering questions such as these. I never envisioned how I would explain my decaying family tree to my children. Their inquisition caught me off guard, but it reminded me that we all want to know where we come from. Just as we count the rings on a tree trunk to determine its age and history, our children ask questions about the details of their family heritage to understand who they are. It's up to us to decide what information we divulge and what information we withhold.

Tara ❀ I want my children to know my story because it's a story of God's provision and grace. I want them to know how blessed they are and that not all children have been given what they have. I want them to know that I credit God's healing for whatever might be good about my marriage and our family. I want them to know that I have chosen to live out forgiveness and grace toward my parents and that none of that happens by accident.

I want you to be more prepared to answer your kids' questions than I was. Most likely your kids will want to know about your childhood—your favorite birthday party, holiday traditions, tree houses and forts you played in as a kid. They'll also want to know about their grandparents, their extended family, and their great big family tree. It's up to you to handle their questions with a balance of truth and grace.

Franny ❀ I have been open and honest with my children. I let them know that I am not perfect and that God is not done with me yet. I make many mistakes, and so will they. I want them to know that I may not always like everything they do, but I am here no matter what path they take. My children have never met the mother who raised me, but I share stories often and let them ask questions.

Ponder the following questions as you prepare for the day your child asks questions about your own childhood. Remember, your audience is your child—not your husband, your counselor, or your friend.

In two to three sentences, describe your family experience while you were growing up. Were your parents together or separated? Were they both a part of your life or not?

What is your favorite childhood memory?

What was difficult about your childhood?

What was your favorite thing to do with your mom or other mother figure when you were a kid?

What was your favorite thing to do with your dad or other father figure when you were a kid?

What do you wish your mom had done differently?

What do wish your dad had done differently?

Were you mostly happy or sad (or something else) as a kid?

If you could change something from your childhood, what would you change?

Decoding the Mother-Child Relationship

Last week I was helping Clarey pick out her clothes for school and asking myself for the sixty-seventh time, *Why don't we do this the night before?*

"Let's narrow it down, Clarey," I said, trying to help her focus. "Athletic or something super cute today?"

"I wanna dress like you," she said with a big smile on her face. My heart about melted. I know she won't always look up to me as she did that morning. I know she won't always want to emulate my look. I know she won't always hold my hand and give me the third-grade gossip, but today I am soaking it up because it hasn't happened without much care and nurturing.

I have spent much time investing in Clarey. We read devotionals together, we talk, we share. She asks questions (and if they're about math, I send her to her dad). I encourage her in her strengths and help her in her weaknesses. We spend time together. We laugh. We cry. We disagree. She misbehaves and receives a consequence. I make mistakes too. I apologize, not enough but more often than I'd like. I am hoping, at the end of the day, that I am giving her the nourishment she needs to grow into the confident woman God intends her to be.

Cultivating a healthy mother-child relationship is a dance of love and discipline, truth and grace, reliance and independence, obedience and trust. Some of my broken branch friends have confided that they missed out on this dance and never felt a deep connection with their own mothers. Now these women are mothers themselves and are pouring into their children to ensure their family tree grows longer, stronger, fuller branches.

Catherine ❋ I always felt that I missed out on the typical mother-daughter relationship. I longed for my mom to be interested in my life or to just go shopping or to dinner with me. I wanted her to care about what I was watching or who I was hanging out with. She trusted me, which was amazing, but because she was so hands-off, I felt that she didn't love me enough to care.

Maybe your mom had a difficult time bonding with you because she was rebuilding her life postdivorce, adjusting to the workforce, recovering from an abusive relationship, or trying to beat an addiction. Whatever her circumstance, children sometimes take second place to the many demands for a mother's time, emotions, and energy. Understanding your mother's history and your relationship with her is key to identifying your insecurities, anxieties, and hopes for today and the future. It will also help you avoid making the same mistakes with your own children.

Maybe you don't have a daughter, but you long to cultivate a close connection with your son. Girls, boys, one child or five, remember this: You might not have had a godly mother, but you can be a godly mother. You might not have had a mother who protected her children, but you can be a mother who protects her children. You might not have had a mother who prayed for you, but you can be a mother who prays for her children.

Describe your relationship with your mom.

How has it affected your parenting?

Parenting Without Role Models

For many women who grew up in dysfunctional families, parenting might feel like gardening without any tools or instructions. We hold seeds in our hands and look down at rich, fertile soil, but we have no idea how to merge the two to create beautiful magnolias and strong oaks.

Catherine ❁ When you have no model for good parenting, you kind of make it up as you go.

Women from dysfunctional families face parenting challenges that include the following:

- Exposure to unhealthy family members
- Fear-based decision-making
- Feelings of lack of control
- High anxiety
- Inability to set boundaries
- No role models
- No support from extended family
- Repeating unhealthy patterns
- Unresolved issues (or baggage)

Place a check mark next to anything from the list above that describes you. How do those things affect your parenting?

We desperately want a different life for our children. Therefore, many of us are overly critical of our parenting. We set our mothering bar at an impossible height and feel like failures when our little sprouts don't meet our expectations.

Or maybe we swing the pendulum in the opposite direction. We over-indulge our children to make up for what we lacked. While our intentions might be pure, this overreaction to our own upbringing will not protect our children from pain and disappointment in the long run—it will just delay it. In actuality, coddling our children produces an entitlement mentality so prevalent in our culture. Not only will obliging our children harm them, but it will cause you to overcommit, overstress, overspend, and overdo it in every aspect of life, all in the name of providing a utopian life for your kids that is really just a façade, as they will discover once they step foot into the real world.

Neither of these approaches is wise, but if we've never seen healthy parenting, we need to give ourselves grace. Then we can equip ourselves to be healthy moms who pursue Jesus and love our children.

First, and most important, we should spend time in God's Word. No book, person, class, or substitute can equip us as our heavenly Father can. When we're confused, tired, spent, overwhelmed, afraid, worried, angry, frustrated, or sad, His Word seeps into our soul and meets our every need. "And my God will meet all your needs according to the riches of his glory in Christ Jesus" (Phil. 4:19).

God also speaks to us and provides for us through people, events, and resources. One way He does this is through mentors. If you did not grow up with healthy parents for role models, a mentor might be a good resource for you. A mentor is a woman in a season of life ahead of you who walks with you through the mothering, marriage, single, widowed, or divorced life jour-ney. Every mentoring relationship looks different, so think about what you want to accomplish. Some women read a book together, others go through a Bible study, and some simply meet for coffee and chat.

Some churches have formal mentoring programs that match you up with another woman. Other mentoring relationships occur more organically, as when a woman you already know meets with you and pours encourage-ment and insight into you. Many women don't think they are equipped to be a mentor—but they are. Or they fear they won't have all the answers—and they won't. But they will have a heart to journey through life with you and share their own experiences of how God led them through difficult times and the wisdom they gained. In God's economy, a humble spirit and a willing heart are more valuable than right answers.

Catherine ❋ I am doing everything I can to build a different relationship with my children, especially with my oldest daughter. She is at an age (ten) where I struggle to connect with her because she is no longer the little, squishy, funny toddler. She is all limbs and elbows and almost as tall as me, and I have to adjust how I talk to her and interact with her—and I have had a hard time. I look to those mamas a few years ahead of me whose relationships with their daughters are what I want to emulate, and I ask them a lot of questions. I have to consciously engage my daughter and hug her and snuggle with her. I ask her tough questions and laugh with her because those are the foundational pieces of the middle school and high school relationship that I want with her.

Another way to equip yourself as you parent is to attend groups such as MOPS (Mothers of Preschoolers), a women's Bible study, a parenting class, or even a seminar through your church or community. These groups fill your well of parenting knowledge while also connecting you to other moms.

One thing that helped me as a mom of young children was joining a playgroup. We said it was to help the kids learn interactive play, but we all knew the group was really to keep the moms sane. We met once a week, and while the kids played, we shared our frustrations, joys, parenting tips, and sometimes prayer requests. I gained great wisdom from watching other mothers with their children, asking questions, and listening to their conversations. Many of those moms are still my closest friends today.

If you don't have time for a playgroup, you and your husband might consider joining a small group through your church. Connecting with a group of other parents in the same stage of life reminds us all that we're not alone. As you share stories and struggles, you laugh, cry, and hopefully form friendships that last for years to come.

Never stop learning. Read books, articles, and blogs pertaining to parenting and the hurdles you face. Ask your children's minister for recommendations.

As a foster mom, I joined a group of other foster moms. Even though we all had other groups of friends, sometimes we needed to vent about caseworkers, attachment disorder, family visits, and other issues that only foster parents could relate to. If you are divorced, remarried, an adoptive mom, or a parent of a special needs child, consider seeking out a support group of other parents in the same situation for support, guidance, and friendship.

Do you currently have a mentor? If so, how has that relationship helped you grow spiritually? If not, who might you ask to mentor you? If you can't think of anyone, are you willing to ask someone on your church staff whom they recommend? Can you commit to begin seeking out a mentor this week?

Creating a Christ-Centered Legacy

Every generation shares one value: we all want to give our children a better life than we experienced. In order to do that, we must determine our family's core values—the Christ-centered standards that define our family and set us apart.

Elyse ✸ I am vigilant in my role as a parent but work hard not to overprotect. I see my children as undeserved gifts, the exemplification of grace. They are joy and rest to my soul. They have helped me die to fears and pride, release control, and embrace the beauty and goodness of God. I see Jesus in them.

Our older three children are each two years apart, and they are both best friends and archenemies. We could create a long list of family rules with dos and don'ts to limit the arguing, but instead, when the bickering swells and chaos ensues, we ask our children these two questions: Are you being kind? and Are you being respectful? Kindness and respect are two of our family's core values.

Hillary ✸ I feel as if I missed out on having a normal childhood and making lots of fun memories. I was extremely shy and quiet, especially during my elementary school years, and I attribute that to the turmoil and chaos that was constantly surrounding me. I never had stability, except when I stayed with my grandparents, and I was always ashamed and embarrassed of my family's dysfunction. I missed out on everyday family life that so many take for granted: sitting around the table and having dinner together, going to church, having friends spend the night, having both parents attend school functions, and feeling safe and secure.

From the time I got married, I knew I wanted to have a marriage and family completely different from what I had experienced as a child. Because of my childhood, I have always been so determined to raise my children the way I wished I had been raised. I want my kids to be happy, to feel safe and secure, and to know they are loved unconditionally. I sometimes think I try too hard to make my children's lives perfect. I want so badly to make sure they have a childhood full of happy times and cherished memories.

You will determine your own family values, but as you do, consider the following priorities.

1. Invest Time

First, we should invest time in our children. Whether it's a simple game of hide-and-go-seek, a trip to the mall, or a game of backyard football, kids want to spend time with their parents. Even when they graduate into the land of puberty and dating, they still want our time (it just switches from Play-Doh and piggyback rides to late-night conversations over a bowl of ice cream). Just remember, kids want your presence and spell *love* T-I-M-E.

Leslie ❀ My dysfunctional relationship with my mom has greatly affected my parenting style. I know she loved me, but I never felt that she liked me. There a difference.

It has always been important to me that my kids know that I like them. Because my mom didn't seem to like me, she also didn't seem to like my friends. Sleepovers were always at my friends' houses, and I always rode with someone else. I was an inconvenience to my mom.

So now, I probably go overboard in doing the opposite with my kids. I try to have conversations with them as often as possible about their interests, their friends, and their school. I pursue knowing them. I always want them to feel that their friends are welcome in our home, and I go out of my way to take them to social engagements. Having a good relationship with each of my kids is very important to me. I don't want my kids to grow up and think I don't know them.

2. Shower Affection

Next, we should never withhold affection from our children. When we have family movie night, I work on my computer—until a gangly body climbs into my lap longing to be held. Physical touch is not my love language, and as a WAHM (work-at-home mom), my work is never done, so it's tempting to set my child next to me and hack away on my keyboard. Then I remember that soon they'll want to spend more time with their friends than with me. Soon they'll be embarrassed to hold my hand in public. So I wrap my arms around my not-so-little-ones and enjoy the show. Never miss out on showering your kids with affection.

3. Encourage and Comfort

Encourage your children in their strengths and comfort them in their weaknesses. I know this may be shocking, but everyone does not deserve a trophy. In life there actually are winners and losers.

As I write this, our older three kids are seven, nine, and eleven, and they are discovering the difficult reality that they won't make every team they try out for, even when they practice. Even when they study, they won't always make an A. They don't all rise to the same level, and that's disappointing for them. As parents, we are helping them navigate their innate, fierce, competitive drives and reminding them that they have God-given strengths and weaknesses. If one makes the soccer team, then that is God's plan for her and the place where she will flourish. If one makes it into the Gifted and Talented program, then that is God's plan for him. The world will build up and then tear down our children with false claims and empty promises. It is our job to instill in them a sense of confidence and identity.

4. Admit Failures

Finally, admit your failures. Apologize. Ask for forgiveness. The other day our sons disappointed us, and without any prompting Carter said, "Mom, can I call Dad at work and apologize?"

I was so proud of him for taking responsibility. But I knew that if he had never seen Brandon and I apologize for our mistakes, he wouldn't have felt safe enough to apologize for his.

> *Karen* ❀ I pray very hard about being gracious and allowing my children to fail. I've given up on not ever raising my voice—it's just not going to happen. The words I speak can never be taken back, so I pray the Lord always keeps that thought in the front of my mind. Apologizing when I've wronged my children and spouse is huge.

After reading these family values, what are some values you would like to instill in your family?

The Memory Keeper

Life is not one-dimensional. Sometimes we get stuck in the self-pity trap and think our life is all hardship and dysfunction. We forget the sweet moments God sprinkled throughout our years.

I recently read *The New York Times* best seller *The Child Called It*, in which a man named David Pelzer recounts his abusive childhood. His nightmare ended when he entered the foster care system at age twelve. Remarkably, even though David almost died several times at the hands of his sadistic, abusive mother; even though his brothers turned against him; and even though his father abandoned him, he was still able to recall happy memories with his family. David's resilience brought him to a place of forgiveness and peace.

It's important to release negative memories and embrace happy memories for our emotional health, but this also helps us honor our families. We don't have to like our families or condone their actions. We don't have to eat dinner or spend holidays with them. But the Bible does call us to honor our parents: "Honor your father and your mother, so that you may live long in the land the Lord your God is giving you" (Exod. 20:12). Remembering even small joyful moments makes honoring our parents easier.

Storing up happy memories also helps as we parent. Our children will ask about our childhood, and while we don't want to paint an unrealistic picture, we do want to balance truth with grace.

The Memory Keeper log found in appendix E will help you do this. Record happy moments and memories from your growing-up years, then refer to this list when you find yourself in a place of despair. (Tip: You might want to make copies of the Memory Keeper log *before you fill it in* so you can add to it as more positive memories surface. Another option is to start your own Memory Keeper log in a journal or notebook.)

Strengthening Your Roots

1. When it comes to your parenting style, do you try to create a utopian environment or a realistic environment for your child that drastically differs from your childhood experience? Describe here.

2. Do you plan to do anything different in your parenting after reading this chapter? Explain.

3. Do you agree with Catherine that, "When you have no model for good parenting, you kind of make it up as you go"? Is this how you approach parenting? Explain.

4. Even if we did not have healthy parenting role models, we can take steps toward intentionally parenting our children in healthy ways by doing the following:

   Reading parenting books

   Seeking a mentor

   Taking parenting classes

   Attending parenting seminars and conferences

   Joining moms groups and playgroups

   Participating in Bible studies and prayer groups

   Connecting with groups that specifically apply to our season of life (e.g., foster parenting, single parenting)

   Out of the above options, circle the one(s) you are currently doing. Put a check mark by the one(s) you will commit to doing over the next three to six months.

5. What lesson did you take away from using the Memory Keeper log?

RECLAIMING YOUR BROKEN BRANCHES

Each one of my friends and fellow broken branches grew up in a less-than-perfect family. Their homes were plagued by abuse, abandonment, divorce, controlling and conditional love, mental illness, addiction, and other painful influences. While most little girls happily played tea parties and dress up, they crept quietly through their childhoods unnoticed (or inappropriately noticed), unprotected, and unloved.

Yet none of these women were forgotten—and neither were you. God's protective hand covered each of them and ushered them into the beautiful lives they live today. Their lives are not free from trials. They have endured many difficulties, yet they weathered these trials because God walked the journey with them. He watches over them, provides for them, and loves them—just as He loves you.

The apostle Paul writes, "We are cracked and chipped from our afflictions on all sides, but we are not crushed by them. We are bewildered at times, but we do not give in to despair. We are persecuted, but we have not been abandoned. We have been knocked down, but we are not destroyed" (2 Cor. 4:8–9 voice). Like Paul, none of us have been abandoned or destroyed.

Hillary ❁ While my young eyes could not see this truth back then, I now realize the Great Rescuer is an expert in restoring and reviving family trees, one small branch at a time. He did it for me, and he can do it for you.

God rescued you for a reason. He rescued you from your broken branches, and He is reclaiming your family tree so you can positively influence your family for generations to come. It's up to you to live a life worthy of His rescue mission.

I asked each of my fellow broken branches to fill in the blank below:

My background has made me _____.

Here are some of their answers:

My background has made me dependent on Christ.
grateful.
humble.
motivated.
realistic.
relational.
resilient.
stronger.
a survivor.

What about you? What influence has your background had on you?

My background has made me _____.

By reading this book, you've taken steps toward healing the broken branches in your family tree—grieving your past, equipping yourself to deal with the present, and building a healthy future for yourself and your loved ones. As you move forward, prayerfully use the knowledge you've gained as a guide to lead you to your next steps of healing and restoration.

Above all else, know that God is for you. And if He is for you, nothing can stand against you (Rom. 8:31).

APPENDIX A

PANDORA'S BOX

Memory	At the Time I Felt . . .	The Enemy's Lie	God's Truth	Now I Feel . . .
My dad forgot my high school graduation.	Sad Angry Disappointed Hurt Worthless	If I were a better daughter—smarter, prettier, more popular—then he would have come. I am worthless.	I am valuable (Luke 12:6–7). God loves me so much and thinks I am worth something; therefore, he purposefully sent his only Son to die in my place (Rom. 5:8). God is my true Father (Ps. 27:10 ESV). God is calling me to forgive my dad (Eph. 4:32).	Sorry for my dad because he chose not to participate in an important life event. He missed out. Grateful for the people God put in my life who support me (my mom, grandparents, friends).

Memory	At the Time I Felt . . .	The Enemy's Lie	God's Truth	Now I Feel . . .

DECONSTRUCTION FOR RECONSTRUCTION

Deconstruction (the baggage I want to leave behind)	Impact (how this behavior affected me or made me feel, or a lie I believed because of it)	God's Truth (restorative power from Jesus Christ)	Reconstruction (my response)
Alcoholism runs rampant throughout my family. My parents are both alcoholics, as is my younger sister, an aunt, and two uncles.	When I was a young child, I thought drinking at holidays, getting loud and "silly," was just adults having fun. But the nights my parents would yell until they passed out—those times were scary. As I got older and understood more, I realized my family's drinking wasn't fun and games. I felt as if they chose drinking and their dysfunctional relationship over creating a healthy home life for us kids.	Scripture says, "See, I am doing a new thing! Now it springs up; do you not perceive it? I am making a way in the wilderness and streams in the wasteland" (Isa. 43:19).	I know that God is breaking the cycle of alcoholism through me. I have no desire to drink, and I don't put myself in situations where there is lots of partying and alcohol. I want to create a healthy, Christ-centered family, free from addiction, and I know Jesus is the only way to do that.

Deconstruction (the baggage I want to leave behind)	Impact (how this behavior affected me or made me feel, or a lie I believed because of it)	God's Truth (restorative power from Jesus Christ)	Reconstruction (my response)

APPENDIX C

GOD'S TRUTH

The following verses are provided to help you complete your "Pandora's Box" and "Deconstruction for Reconstruction" charts.

Comfort	Finances	Forgiveness
Psalm 23:4	Proverbs 22:7	Daniel 9:9
Psalm 27:1	Proverbs 28:6	Matthew 6:14–15
Psalm 34:18	Ephesians 4:32	2 Corinthians 5:17
John 14:26–27	Hebrews 13:5	Ephesians 4:32
God's Plan	**Grace**	**Humility**
Proverbs 3:5–6	John 1:14	Isaiah 5:21
Proverbs 16:9	2 Corinthians 12:8–9	Romans 12:3
Ecclesiastes 3:1–22	Ephesians 2:8–9	Ephesians 4:2
Jeremiah 29:11	James 4:6	James 4:10
Love	**Not Abandoned or Forsaken**	**Peace**
Proverbs 10:12	Joshua 1:9	John 16:33
Jeremiah 31:3	Psalm 27:10	Galatians 5:22
Mark 12:30–31	John 6:37	James 3:18
Hebrews 13:1–3	Hebrews 13:5	1 Peter 5:7
Prayer	**Significance / Self-Worth**	**Sin**
Jeremiah 29:12	1 Samuel 16:7	Psalm 119:133
Matthew 7:7	Psalm 139:13–15	Matthew 7:3
Ephesians 6:18	Isaiah 43:4	Romans 3:23
1 John 5:14	Luke 12:6–7	Romans 6:15

Salvation	Self-Control	Temptation
John 3:16–17	Proverbs 19:11	Matthew 26:41
John 14:6	Proverbs 25:28	Mark 14:38
Romans 5:8	Proverbs 29:11	1 Corinthians 10:13
Titus 3:5	Galatians 5:22–23	Hebrews 2:18
Worry / Fear		
Psalm 55:22		
Psalm 112:7		
Matthew 6:31–34		
Isaiah 41:10		

SEVENTY TIMES SEVEN FORGIVENESS CHART

Who Do I Need to Forgive?	What Did This Person Do to Me?	How Did This Make Me Feel at the Time?	How Did I Respond at the Time? Was It a Biblical Response?	How Does It Make Me Feel Today?	Is God Calling Me to Forgive? To Reconcile?
My dad and brother	Constantly criticized me for my weight.	It made me feel worthless and rejected.	I tried to disappear. I became a wallflower at school and at home. I tried to stay out of everyone's way so they wouldn't notice me. I thought if I could go unnoticed, then they would leave me alone. But that trick never worked.	Today I am slowly realizing my value is in Jesus, not in my family's opinion of me. But it is still difficult. Their words are stuck in my head, and it's difficult to turn off their voices.	I have forgiven them, although it is a daily choice. Every time a memory creeps into my mind, I have to forgive all over again. Every time I go swimsuit shopping and remember those awful summers at the family lake house, I have to forgive all over again. I have to keep a healthy distance from them because they still don't understand how their words have hurt me. They think I am overly sensitive and continue to make remarks even today. Reconciliation is not possible because they don't think they have done anything wrong.

Who Do I Need to Forgive?	What Did This Person Do to Me?	How Did This Make Me Feel at the Time?	How Did I Respond at the Time? Was It a Biblical Response?	How Does It Make Me Feel Today?	Is God Calling Me to Forgive? To Reconcile?

APPENDIX E

MEMORY KEEPER

Memory	At the Time I Felt . . .	Now I Feel . . .	Prayer to God
My mom always sang a special song to me before bed.	Safe and loved.	Like that is a tradition I want to carry on when I have kids one day.	God, thank you for this sweet memory. Although times weren't always so calm, I thank you for this tender moment that I can hold on to.

Memory	At the Time I Felt . . .	Now I Feel . . .	Prayer to God

NOTES

Chapter 1: Deep Roots

1. Esme Fuller-Thomson and Angela D. Dalton, "Suicide Ideation Among Individuals Whose Parents Have Divorced: Findings from a Representative Canadian Community Survey," *Psychiatry Research* 187, no. 1–2 (2011): 150–55, doi: http://dx.doi.org/10.1016/j.psychres.2010.12.004.
2. For an easy online Bible study tool, visit BibleGateway.com. You might also consider investing in a parallel Bible that features multiple translations side by side, such as the New King James Version, English Standard Version, or the New American Standard Bible.
3. Corrie Ten Boom, *The Hiding Place* (Peabody, MA: Hendrickson, 2009), 17.
4. Lois Lowry, *The Giver* (New York: Houghton Mifflin, 2014), 193.

Chapter 2: The Pruning Process

1. Jean M. Twenge, *Generation Me: Why Today's Young Americans Are More Confident, Assertive, Entitled—and More Miserable Than Ever Before* (New York: Free Press, 2006), 152.

Chapter 4: Feeding Your Faith

1. Melinda Smith, Robert Segal, and Jeanne Segal, "Depression Symptoms and Warning Signs: Recognizing Depression and Getting the Help You Need," HelpGuide.org, April 2017, https://www.helpguide.org/articles/depression/depression-symptoms-and-warning-signs.htm.
2. "Depression: Fact Sheet," World Health Organization, February 2017, http://www.who.int/mediacentre/factsheets/fs369/en/.
3. Jeanne McCauley et al., "Clinical Characteristics of Women with a History of Childhood Abuse: Unhealed Wounds," *JAMA* 277, no. 17 (1997): 1362–68, doi: 10.1001/jama.1997.03540410040028.
4. Shanta R. Dube et al., "Childhood Abuse, Household Dysfunction, and the Risk of Attempted Suicide Throughout the Life Span: Findings from the Adverse Childhood Experiences Study," *JAMA* 286, no. 24 (2001): 3089–96, doi: 10.1001/jama.286.24.3089.

5. Renee D. Goodwin and Murray B. Stein, "Association Between Childhood Trauma and Physical Disorders Among Adults in the United States," *Psychological Medicine* 34, no. 3 (2004): 509–20, doi: https://doi.org/10.1017/S0033 29170300134X.

6. Charles F. Gillespie and Charles B. Nemeroff, "Early Life Stress and Depression: Childhood Trauma May Lead to Neurobiologically Unique Mood Disorders," *Current Psychiatry* 4, no. 10 (2005): 15–30.

7. Ibid.

8. Ibid.

9. Andreas Maercker et al., "Age of Traumatisation as a Predictor of Post-Traumatic Stress Disorder or Major Depression in Young Women," *British Journal of Psychiatry* 184, no. 6 (2004): 482–87, doi: 10.1192/bjp.184.6.482.

10. Mark Harris, *A Jesus for Generation X: A Place for Faith in a Post-Christian Age* (Richmond, BC: Inter-Varsity Christian Fellowship of Canada, 1997), 4.

Chapter 6: The Garden Gate

1. This list has largely been compiled from the following sources: Henry Cloud and John Townsend, "Adults Without Boundaries Raise Kids Without Boundaries," BoundariesBooks.com, March 15, 2016, http://www.boundaries books.com/boundaries-with-kids/adults-without-boundaries-raise -kids-without-boundaries/; Mark Dombeck, "Boundaries and Dysfunctional Family Systems," MentalHelp.net, August 1, 2006, https://www.mentalhelp .net/articles/boundaries-and-dysfunctional-family-systems/; and Thomas F. Fischer, "Ten Commandments of Dysfunctional Families," MinistryHealth .net, accessed November 16, 2017, http://www.ministryhealth.net/mh_articles /064_ten_commandments_of_dysfunctional_families.html.

2. Michael Dorris, *A Yellow Raft in Blue Water: A Novel* (New York: Picador, 1987), 26.

3. Shahram Heshmat, "Why Do We Remember Certain Things, But Forget Others?" Psychology Today, October 8, 2015, https://www.psychologytoday .com/blog/science-choice/201510/why-do-we-remember-certain-things -forget-others.

4. Thomas L. Constable, "Notes on Exodus: 2017 Edition," Sonic Light, accessed November 16, 2017, 128–9, http://www.soniclight.com/constable/notes/pdf /exodus.pdf.

Chapter 7: A Beautiful Arrangement

1. Barna Group, "New Marriage and Divorce Statistics Released," March 31, 2008,

https://www.barna.org/barna-update/family-kids/42-new-marriage-and
-divorce-statistics-released#.VqQ7tLSsD4c.

2. Jonel Aleccia, "'The New Normal': Cohabitation on the Rise, Study Finds," NBC News, April 4, 2013, http://www.nbcnews.com/health/health-news /new-normal-cohabitation-rise-study-finds-f1C9208429.

Chapter 9: A Whisper in the Wind

1. Leon Morris, *Expository Reflections on the Letter to the Ephesians* (Grand Rapids: Baker, 1994), 146.

Chapter 10: The Calm After the Storm

1. Scott Stanley et al., *A Lasting Promise: The Christian Guide to Fighting for Your Marriage*, 2nd ed (San Francisco: Jossey-Bass Publishers, 2014), 76–79.

Chapter 11: Your Private Garden

1. Kevin Leman, *Sheet Music: Uncovering the Secrets of Sexual Intimacy in Marriage* (Carol Stream, IL: Tyndale, 2008), 30.

2. Enid Gruber and Joel W. Grube, "Adolescent Sexuality and the Media: A Review of Current Knowledge and Implications." *Western Journal of Medicine* 172, no. 3 (2000): 210–14, https://www.ncbi.nlm.nih.gov/pmc/articles/PMC 1070813/.

3. Carolyn C. Ross, "Overexposed and Under-Prepared: The Effects of Early Exposure to Sexual Content," Psychology Today, August 13, 2012, https://www .psychologytoday.com/blog/real-healing/201208/overexposed-and-under -prepared-the-effects-early-exposure-sexual-content.

4. Ibid.

5. Ibid.

6. Ibid.

7. Chris Morris, "Things Are Looking Up in America's Porn Industry," NBC News, January 20, 2015, http://www.nbcnews.com/business/business-news /things-are-looking-americas-porn-industry-n289431.

8. Ross, "Overexposed and Under-Prepared."

9. John Guidubaldi, Joseph D. Perry, and Bonnie K. Nastasi, "Growing Up in a Divorced Family: Initial and Long-Term Perspectives on Children's Adjustment," *Applied Social Psychology Annual* 7 (1987): 202–37, http://psycnet.apa .org/psycinfo/1988-16562-001.

10. Mary Anna Powell and Toby L. Parcel, "Effects of Family Structure on the

Earnings Attainment Process: Differences by Gender," *Journal of Marriage and Family* 59, no. 2 (1997): 421, doi: 10.2307/353480. See also Kathleen E. Kiernan, "Teenage Marriage and Marital Breakdown: A Longitudinal Study," *Population Studies* 40, no. 1 (1986): 35–54, http://www.jstor.org/stable/2174278.

11. Frances K. Goldscheider and Calvin Goldscheider, "The Effects of Childhood Family Structure on Leaving and Returning Home," *Journal of Marriage and the Family* 60, no. 3 (1998): 755, doi: 10.2307/353543.

12. Jill N. Kearns-Bodkin and Kenneth E. Leonard, "Relationship Functioning Among Adult Children of Alcoholics." *Journal of Studies on Alcohol and Drugs* 69, no. 6 (2008): 941–50, www.ncbi.nlm.nih.gov/pmc/articles/PMC2583382/.

13. David Sack, "5 Things Standing Between You and a Healthy Relationship," *Huffington Post*, February 15, 2013, www.huffingtonpost.com/david-sack-md/relationship-advice_b_2686081.html.

Chapter 12: Living Water

1. Shaunti Feldhahn, *The Surprising Secrets of Highly Happy Marriages: The Little Things That Make a Big Difference* (Colorado Springs: Multnomah, 2013), 177–78.

Chapter 13: Graceful Growth

1. Henry Cloud and John Townsend, *Boundaries: When to Say Yes, When to Say No to Take Control of Your Life*, rev. ed. (Grand Rapids: Zondervan, 1992), 140–41.

Chapter 14: Healthy Soil for Growth

1. Judith S. Wallerstein, Judith M. Lewis, and Sandra Blakeslee, *The Unexpected Legacy of Divorce: The 25 Year Landmark Study* (New York: Hachette Books, 2001), 143.

2. Vincent. J. Felitti and Robert F. Anda, "The Relationship of Adverse Childhood Experiences to Adult Medical Disease, Psychiatric Disorders, and Sexual Behavior: Implications for Healthcare," in *The Impact of Early Life Trauma on Health and Disease: The Hidden Epidemic*, ed. Ruth A. Lanius, Eric Vermetten, and Clare Pain (New York: Cambridge University Press, 2010), 77.

3. Ibid., 80.

4. Ibid., 79.